THIRTY-ONE DAYS

JULY AUGUST DECEMBER

POETHICS OBLIVION STAREYES - DARK SUN

authorHOUSE®

AuthorHouse™
1663 Liberty Drive
Bloomington, IN 47403
www.authorhouse.com
Phone: 1-800-839-8640

Published by AuthorHouse 7/16/2012

ISBN: 978-1-4685-9639-7 (sc)
ISBN: 978-1-4772-0299-9 (e)

Contents

COMMISSION TO GAME

POLITICAL BLACKNESS ^{Dark Sun}

This country tills to the - Great land of victory – Let freedom ring!

******

The stance of the black man in this country supposed to be derived from Negro suffrage.

You know the brothers walked to achieve great things for the colored.

However, today it is to be discovered that the brothers are working undercover to keep black people in poorness and the colored was really no part of the Civil Rights Movement.

Negro poorness, it seems, is forever to be seen as colored keeping the dream.

NAACP is still in existence because it represents the falsification of what was gained in a movement that involved non-violence.

War should have transpired and because it did not, the black man has become [**more**] mollified and participates against his people, carrying out the white man crimes.

Standing for better living is not evident to Blackness in America.

White Americans tend to systematically hinder those that are colored via a family lens.

Meaning, if your family isn't for you, you will never succeed in a profile country of inequity.

Your identity is smothered and your attainment becomes never.

Therefore,

you are no one in a country that states opportunity will come.

Nonetheless, you have your belief in God.

You have stood now for your rights and everything in your material world has been sacrificed.

Nevertheless, a greater accomplishment did come.

This is because you believed in God.

MESTIZO: INDIAN-NEGRO!

TROUBLED I SHALL NOT BE. PAIN IS ILLUSIVE. BUT I KNOW THAT I AM ONLY AN HUMAN BEING. DON'T INDUCE ME!

I MUST STAND TALL AND NOT BECOME A STUMP FOR Y'ALL. THIS IS BECAUSE I KNEW WHO CALL ME WITHIN MY MOTHER'S WOMB AND SAID UNTO ME THAT YOU SHALL BE A GIRL AND YOUR EXISTENCE IS NOW!

The greater the gift – The powerful the presence becomes.

Encourage, try not to provoke. Stimulate, try not to dissuade. Tempt – what's wrong with a little temptation? Generating – That's how I will persuade you. Philosophy is creativity in the making. Bringing ideas to a cause, initiating what has been brought forth. If we can produce many more the same way, we have developed innovation and creativity that will be here in the last days. An economy has been made.

Know that profit is money in your pocket – Non-profit is money in the bank but both tend to be the same!

Have you ever been on an emotional high? Where you felt you were on cloud nine? You saw water and fire. Well, I'll tell you. You were in the spirit and I will encourage you to develop that feeling for your ultimate fulfillment! Do you remember how it felt? Well, that is what is sacred to your soul. Therefore, I will now disengage and move on.

In the eyes of my Master, which and who is The Almighty God, I seek solitude and a safe haven when I have no friends to play with and no family to be a part of.

Amen I say unto *The Man* of all Mankind – *Jehovah God Lord*!

COMMISSION TO GAME

Who's that knocking at my door?
Want to come over?
I don't feel like dealing with folks when I have a hangover?
I have to make time for you in my life but last night I just had a real
good time!

Do you understand that sisters and brothers?
Ain't trying to ignore you however...
But I have to get over this hangover.

Why the noise with the dogs?
Can't get next to me?
The next time around you bring domestic violence.
Hit against my window, running down your stairs, and no one seems to
care!
I didn't say anything about it as well.

Understood what you meant brothers.
Not here as pretense sisters.
You seem to have me covered with what you do for a living.
Maybe, it's truly not a misgiving!

Why the concern about the missing panel?
You seem to want to handle me.
You could be my man but you scared to take a stance.
And, I know I just got over my hangover.

Understanding y'all; didn't want you to fall in love with me though!
You know this is my life and I don't have to win and didn't you know?
Jehovah God Lord gave this life only to me men.
Just shut you out of my lifestyle and after a while we will be a thousand
miles apart.
No longer will I have to consider who you seem to think you are.

Commission to *game* but truly not playing with girl or boy, sister or brother, backwards or forward...
In the frame of male or female, just running water crying inside and don't know it because I am in every faucet in society, causing your brain to be dead - no longer a thinking cap residing in your head.
Just a closure of a game and the beginning of **Woman**!

1. *[As the truth unfolds, **Woman** has become the centerfold of gaming and her name is known to be: **Poethics Oblivion Stareyes** and she is a poet laureate – poet scholar!]*

VESTED

****

Overdose is not the prognosis of what will happen.
Laborious to the intellect when there is no reason to kill oneself.
But if done anyway, God speed be with you.
Your best apprehension is to pay attention to your stressors and
wake-up in the morning saying I really didn't kill myself.
I'm vested!
****

I know how that feels **Ramesh**.
However, is it you or your penis?
I know how to strip you of your ego.
So
Don't manifest at my front door.
You are just my spiritual lover. You know!
Not playing games.
You really are the man my vagina yawns for.
You state I am a tease by how you receive me manly.
You were the ram.
We bump heads.
Did you win?
I shall not taunt because I don't want to front.
I really desire you, **Dr. Madhavan**.
When we met it was in April.
Your caveman form was very explosive; however, your tactics
were not over dosive.
Just your bomb shelled.
But our secret love affair will not let it explode; disallowing your
damnation in Hell.
Satan cannot have your soul.
Games are not played between us.
We know what's up.
And, you and I are combustible to our knowledge.

Spiritual leaders of others in the game of love, if only we could be together, who could separate us?

2. [*A discovery of real time in which mankind has developed and implemented via another medium in mentality called spiritual reality. Maybe one day someone will address Poethics. If not so, this will become global neglect and sunken intellect. Money wasted by men and women because they fear the truth and the faculties this truth can create and, therefore, implemented by what has develop.*]

SHOULD I HAVE BEEN

****

In life, we must change!
Try to be ahead things.
Grow from our mistakes to know what's at stake.
****

A holy man was walking.
His cane was in his left hand.
He is mumbling to himself.
What he said was: *"God will make a way out of no way and God knows best!"*

Love is only a feeling.
However, it can be quite fulfilling.
Time tests all of us.
Love is of essence.
Share your life as if it is your last days.
And, maybe it will happen again if and when this one ends.

A woman who never had a lover proclaims to all that she was a virgin.
Never experiencing passion in her life...
Sadness filled the man eyes as he listens and thinks.
[*This woman lies*].
In the entity where she's from, love was done in darkness.
Her problem was a lack of feeling.
The man touches her on the shoulder, as she felt her vagina hang open.

If your living is the misgiving, don't begin to cry.
Hold close to your creator and your maybes will disappear as your life preservers.
It may seem as if there is no reason to think positive.

However, remember…

The Lord provides for all of us.
Your job is to past his assessment of your life in which that is why you are here, as an enjoyment model for The Lord to share with man and his kind.
Claim immortality as the eternal domain and state in this instance that Jehovah God Lord is offered the reminiscence of the crystal ball of life mortal, when the world comes to an end and immortality begins.

3. [*The tribulation of my suffering is misfortune to who I am. The problem is my hardship isn't real. Man and his kind desires to utilize me for free. However, I am not in pain but it is quite difficulty not to cry because the misery is laced in my eyes. Distressed to the world's ordeal and you know, brothers and sisters, I have nothing to give! I must live as a diamond in the ruff. No crimes have I committed. Tell the police they will never handcuff me for any criminal activity.*]

****

Basically I thought so much of you.
But, really you thought too little of yourself.
You claim our friendship ended because you heard the derogatory
statements I said.
However, where they about you?
You haven't mentioned that yet.

****

MAXINE [QUEASY QUEEN BEING]

SHE IS A LADY THAT I KNOW VERY WELL.
SHE FIGURES SHE KNOWS ME AS WELL.
OUR IDENTITIES SEEM TO BE SIMILAR BUT WE REALLY
ARE NOT ALIKE.
IT JUST APPEARS AS APPREHENSION OF WHO WE ARE
AS WELL AS HOW WE ARE PRECEIVED IN THIS LIFE.

YOUR NAME IS MAXINE.
MINE IS THE SAME.
WE ARE WOMEN APPARENTLY.
AS MEN STAND AND STARE AT US, WE PREPARE
OURSELVES FOR THIS IDENTITY.

HE IS A GENTLEMAN THAT KNOWS MANY PEOPLE VERY
WELL.
HE SEEMS TO FIGURE THEY KNOW HIM AS WELL.
A PUBLIC ARENA HE LIVES IN.
STATING HE LOVES THE CROWDS HE'S WITHIN.

MAXINE IS HIS WOMAN.
SHE LOVES HIM LIKE SHE HAS LOVED NO OTHER.
HOWEVER, HE DOES NOT LOVE AS HARD.

MAYBE, BECAUSE HE SEES ME ALSO...

MUST I TELL YOU THAT I AM MAXINE INNER BEING VIRTUALLY.
SO HER NAME MUST BE MINES AS WELL.
SHE DESIRES THIS MAN BUT I KNOW HE IS NOT FOR REAL.
HER MIND IS NOT WEAK AND HER THINKING IS QUITE KEEN.
THEREFORE, SHE MAY FIGURE THIS OUT HERSELF.

THERE ARE MANY OBSTACLES FOR HER TO CROSS TO GAIN HER
LIFE FROM SURREALITY.
CONSEQUENTLY, MAXINE HAS BEEN IMPLANTED INTO REALITY;
HOWEVER, DOES SHE KNOW THIS?
NEVERTHELESS, SHE DOES NOT HAVE HER OWN MIND BECAUSE
HER BRAIN IS WIRED.
NO AWARENESS DOES SHE HAVE OF THIS AND SHE NEVER WILL.
SHE HAS NORMAL INTELLIGENCE WITH HIGH APTITUDE AND
POTENTIAL.
TO DESCRIBE MAXINE, NO ONE WOULD BE ABLE TO.
HER BEAUTY IS ILLUSIVE AND WHEN PICTURES ARE TAKEN OF HER
THEY ARE MISCONSTRUED IN WHICH SHE IS REAL BEAUTIFUL LIKE ME OR
YOU.

MAXINE, MAXINE, MAXINE – ONE OF QUEASY QUEEN BEINGS!
A MAZE OR AMAZING - EXCERPT FROM THE *LABYRINTH* BUT
WRITTEN FOUR YEARS LATER.

4. **[The Labyrinth a mazes most of us and in amazement one
can solve the puzzle of Maxine life, finishing her history
book].**

PARADISE

Lucifer Satan I am not but I keep a hot cunt.
Maybe my daddy in disguise because they state I have sultry
eyes.

Evil lurks in my thoughts about how to get men penis off
without having sex in this mental medium I live within.
Why has this been done?
I'm trying to discover that through my words – through my
Book of Psalms.

The Devil is not me.
My pussy is human being, which is not part of a wicked entity.
However, I have you to know that down the valley of my tits is
lava.
Want to lick them?
They won't burn your tongue only making you want to taste my
cum.

Do I turn you on?
That's what I'm here for.
Sex has been done for real boy and I am as fresh as I can be.
Now, you really desire me.

An evil life form is not my persona.
My body is just insatiable.
If you wish for me, I will know.
Your mind will become misconstrued because I will begin to
covet.
Voices in your brain I will create.

This is not the end to my yearning.
I will be here forever.
Listen to what I say and our entity will be made [This day!].

5. *[As part of the mind, I will create a sexual paradise that enables you to live a heterosexual lifestyle. Men will envy you because you are my child.]*

QUANDARY

Opening the window for a breeze…
Dogs are barking!
My mind is only on me.
Relaxing…

As my story of the day unfolds, someone knocks.
Startling me, I hurry to the front door.
There stands an image of long-ago.
We hug and I let him in.
I begin to remember how deeply in love I was with this man.
But our destinies had to part and I left with my heart.

We talked for hours.
No intimacy transpired between us because we knew our lives
was not fair to us and therefore, we did not desire any closeness.
Just reminiscence of tragedy we had went through for healing
purposes on this three-year Anniversary.

***

What happen?
You may ask.
This is the tale as is.

***

His mother desired to be me.
So she set out to steal my identity.
In darkness she laid in our bed waiting on Ted.
A man entered the room and she presumed her man had come
home.
Voicing that she was there, my stalker shot her three times in
the head.
The bullets were for me.

In irony, she had really stolen my identity.
He shot himself as well ending my dilemma.

The police came on the screen afraid that it was me.
Ted and I played it off.
He had told me his ordeal with his mother as a teenager.

He was the star athlete at our high school.
His mother was unstable and desired him for her sex tool.
She will explain that this would keep them close but he could not tell anyone.
His grandmother on his father side had fill Ted in on his mother family history of incest.
Ted figured he did not want any part of that mess.
So he asked his father could he live with him but he also keep in contact with his mother because of his sister and baby brother.
His father said yes to Ted and asked his other kids did they want to live with him as well.
It so happen that his sister was close to their mother and his baby brother was also.
So they said no.

Ted graduated from high school as valedictorian of his class and his body was explosive.
Ted was fine as he could be.
He now could communicate with his mother without her approaching him for sex.
He had not told his father of this but had kept this to himself.
Nevertheless, his mother, in secret, still desired her son.

Ted and I started dating in high school.
I was familiar with his family through us living in the same metropolitan city, however, not in the same community.
We end up going to the same university in the city we lived in and our relationship flourished.

We moved into our apartment while we were in college and his mother use to come over.
And now, three years later, we remember the tragedy.
Ted cries out to me and I answered.
We are bonded by our relationship but not by marriage.
He has successfully conquered his demons and mine disappear on that night of my stalker killing himself.

Ted mother was wealthy and I knew that she only was nice to me because of Ted.
The police discover she had paid my stalker to pursue me as his prey.
Ted has been told this as well and he stated that is why his mother is dead in which he says quietly to himself: **"This ends this horrid tale."**

6. [*Queasy Queen Beings and they do not know anything of it. Ted is Queasy Queen's son and he has her powers. He would have acquired his mother's powers without help, which would have been through incest before forty. However, incest did not happen between Ted and his mother, Queasy Queen, and therefore, he will acquire her powers at the age of forty (40). His sister and brother have theirs but did not divulge because there mother had explain theirs to them when she bestowed. Telling Ted's sister, Harmony, at ten (10) what she was doing as she assisted her in getting dressed, which was lesser than incest. she kissed her vagina. Telling Ted's brother, Destine, at fifteen (15), when she gave him a kiss as he was leaving why she tongued him, which was lesser than incest. Incest was only for Ted because he was the oldest and her first born. His grandmother on his father side knew nothing of this because she was human and disagreed with incest openly. More so, this was unheard of through an entity of the government.*]

SABIEN ALLEGRA BALDWIN & ALEXIS ROCHELLE-MARIE BALDWIN

****

YOU HAVE NOT DONE ANYTHING TO ANYONE BUT YOURSELF.
HOPEFULLY YOU WILL FIND IT IN YOUR INTELLECT HOW TO CORRECT YOUR MESS.
IF NOT, THEN THERE'S NOTHING LEFT.

****

Sabien saw spirits as a child.
His mother told him he had a veil over his eyes.!
He became quite afraid and he never told his mother when he saw them again.
He kept his fears within.

As he grew older, he discovered warlocking.
He developed spells to cast in his paradise.
Not from a book but from his mind…
Many thought he was as smart as Albert Einstein.

Sabien became very successful in life with his life work being private investigation.
He solved cases without any hesitation and he did not procrastinate when he divulged what was at stake or the mistakes that were made to end the charade.

He married at the age of thirty-three (33).
Having six (6) kids and now the oldest had turned eighteen (18) in which the youngest was five and saw spirits at night.
Sabien told her as his mother had told him; she had a veil over her eyes.
Alexis did not understand and she told her father over and over again.

By doing this, she released the demons from hell and this was travesty of the mind to her father because he did not tell his mother over and over again about the spirits he saw as a child as well.

Sabien and his daughter became very close.
His other children thought that she was his favorite.
However, she was not.
Sabien felt and had the same level of love for all his children.
It was just Alexis would be brilliant and Sabien's other five children would be as smart as their father.

The demons that Sabien lived with was Alexis's inner beings. By telling her father over and over again about the spirits she witness, she restricted these demons from infiltrating her sending them to her father's warlock world.

In afterlife, this mental paradise is where Sabien soul would go and when his wife and children died their souls would go there also.
If Sabien lived to see any his son-in-laws or daughter-in-laws and any his grandchildren, their souls would be sent to this world too regardless of how things ended.

These are the names of Sabien and Loretta Baldwin kids:

Fabien Alavont Baldwin– Eighteen (18) Years Old
Sabien Allegra Baldwin II – Sixteen (16) Years Old
Harmonica Deontia Baldwin – Twelve (12) Years old
Brittany Maria Baldwin – Ten (10) Years Old
Felix Lalegra Baldwin – Ten (10) Years old
Alexis Rochelle-Marie Baldwin – Five (5) Years old

7. *[Each of Sabien and Loretta Baldwin kids has spiritual powers. Throughout this book the author will tell about them.]*

POETHICS OBLIVION STAREYES

I want the world to believe that I'm a Lesbian.
So the man I desire must be a transvestite.
Camouflaging his identity day and night [when he's with me]...
I know I have the man to fit my fantasy, not a fetish but passion
to deep for psychology.

His name is Hardik Shah.
He's olive complexion, very sexy, as handsome as any man can
be.
He thrills me.
However, I know to take this slow to avoid rejection.
He will be seduced by me through him being my physician.

[****]

Dr. Shah will come to me at night via my wardrobe.
A beautiful woman he shall be as I undress him, revealing my
treasure – his torso and his penis.
I am so excited.
The love we are about to make is earth shaking and my body is
quaking for sexual fulfillment that Hardik can only give [me].

My name is *POETHICS OBLIVION STAREYES*.

8. *[Therefore, I must remain single. This is a spiritual marriage
   and Hardik completes my sexual identity. No other desires I
   have and we're together until life transpires.]*

PCP

Must I deal with Annette Aquino?
She seems too really care though.
Is it just me with my science of human beings lens on or am I in
a judgment mode?
I know I see people as people and not within their race or
nationality unless culture is the mentality.
So what is it?
Can I analyze?
Will it become scrutiny?
Making Dr. Annette Aquino my enmity?

One of the males from Boyz II Men was her in another medium
at Eastpointe Family Physicians?
Not to mention her husband, who when I visit, has his office
visits as well.
Is he concern for her in the event she tells me what is happening
when I come there?
Maybe that is it?
However, Annette does not divulge any information.

Deal or no deal is specifically how it is.
I must keep her in my life now until I leave here.
She is my Primary Care Physician [PCP], as you all know.
So, Dr. Annette Aquino is my PCP and for next two (2) years
that's the way it shall be.

9. **[Am I in a danger zone or is this my medical home? I will
only know by not changing my PCP from Annette Aquino,
MD.]**

{Note: Dr. Aquino stop being my primary physician in March 2010.}

<u>Verlena</u>, <u>I'll Be Right In</u>.

Just as nice as she can be
Jamie!
This is Dr. Shah assistant.
Is she a pretense?
No, I believe this is her personality?
Let me test!
In this mental medium that I'm in in Southeastern Michigan,
Jamie is visible to me when I am not there for an office visit.
Usually it happens right after I visit Dr. Shah for Pain Therapy.
He gives me my adjustments and she writes the notes.
The environment is real volatile but I ignore.
Why do I ignore - because I refuse to visit every doctor here in
Southeastern Michigan.
"Jamie is going to change you to another room" states
another MA.
She takes my blood pressure and temperature, talks nicely to me
and then, Jamie changes me to another room.
In comes Dr. Shah, as fine as he can be.
But I was thinking Jamie would be in to Prep me for his entry.
However, he came directly instead trying to mess with my head.
Nevertheless, he did not succeed.
He has to do more than that to get next to me.
He's trying to take my identity.
I know he knows I write Poetry.
I recently wrote one about him with me in a fantasy.
Jamie knows as well.
She is his main squeeze out of the office MAs because she
always takes his notes when he provides me with therapy.
To make this so definite, she calls me to remain me of my
appointments.
Dr. Shah and Jamie, a mixture of the same that is what she said
when she voiced to me: **"Verlena, I will be right in."**

10. [Well Dr. Shah ever fulfill my fantasy when he adjusts me? Can I make him a part of my destiny?]

1969

Give me your tired your poor your hurdled masses yawning to
breathe free!

****

This empty space is where my heart resides.
No love do I have inside.
I have been hurt by to many men and women, I do not desire.

****

If they knew what I thought, they would not bother to fight.
I'll become rich overnight because I am their way of life.
Why will they not settle?
It's not a claim that they can deny.
They must compensate this worker for what they have done to
her life.

Emptiness is only a space in this body of mine.
Men are subjected in losing their minds.
Women projection is that of the insane because I am truly
commission to game.

Thinking why they do not know my thoughts when they are the
cause of them all.
Male and female really are a hollow being because of how they
believe they have proceeded me.
They will pay this worker.
They really have not a choice.
However, if they don't, I will take it to the Supreme Court.
This is the hole they live in.
An abyss that has no enduring until I win and their settlement is
this nation's curing.

There's a break in society that must unite.
And I am the life that separates even though they claim to be the
United States.
Law enforcement is the tragedy.
Rap Music allegation of badness.
All know - just a state of madness.
Contention has it that the muvee will win.
The sadness is he already has.
Declare what {White} men have set out to achieve as power
over women until the end of eternity.

This is 1969.

11. **[President Lydon Baines Johnson asked for the tired and poor hurdled in masses that was yawning to breathe free. Who was he referring to? The answer is the immigrants that neutralize to this country – the United States of America. Why when his ancestor President George Washington proclaimed neutralization from other countries problems, which we know as citizens of United States of America that just may be that country's people. No ill feelings meant naturalized people.]**

Somewhere In Africa

I'm gonna go an live in Africa.
Visit the Jungle like Hanna.
Maybe have me a zoo at my home like Michael Jackson.
Being Indian-Negro, I feel the need to visit my maternal grandfather homeland.
Pilgrimage is what this is called.
To my ancestral terrain, I must go.

You know South Africa made a holy connection when I was a child.
Through mass communication of a broadcasting station, they sent me a link, which attached itself to my thoracic spine.
In relation to what is happening in my life now, Africa is my only ally.

When I get to Africa, I'm gonna live in the west.
That is definite to my maternal grandfather heritage.
I'm gonna top soil and build me a mansion like those in the north and everyone will ask – "**Where is she really from**?"
And when you know anything, I will have settled a Village and there will be people a plenty.
We will develop an economy, making this part of West Africa a metropolitan city.

Knowledge is to Libya and how it could have been established.
Nevertheless, it was not.
Therefore, I am here to change that.
West Africa is calling me and I must answer.

Another Dubai made, imagery from my brain.
Let's join together to make this a reality in humanity.
And, then we will do it once again - *Somewhere In Africa*.

12. **[Fredrick Douglas refused Libya during slavery time. Thus, *Somewhere in Africa* will capture the mind if and**

when you are still diaspora though the stories of your ancestors.]

MIMESIS

****

He told me if I get up to 400 pounds he would have sex with me.
His name is Michael Jordan.
White women call him M.J.
The mistake he made.

****

To live in sexual oppression is sort of absurd.
Many men have done that to themselves.
Because of the white man, black man, and olive technology, they cannot
make love to me.
I am Poethics.

And now they are constantly trying to achieve the impossible
through the word sex when they cannot have this.
White women tell them to keep it simple.
Black women state I will never again have a real life.
An olive believes that I am the sacrifice.
All stating that I am susceptible to anything they do to me in life.

But why did M.J. state he would make love to me if I weighed 400
pounds?
I do now, actually, somewhat more.
Nevertheless, M.J. is not knocking at my door.

A mysterious weight gain I have that came from nowhere.
Evidently to get Michael Jordon's attention so that he could ask me for
mine.

Now it is time for me to lose weight and the mystery of it all is
that I am not walking in anybody's life but my own.

Therefore, I let you know the name of this piece of poetry is mimesis. Can you figure out the meaning of this?

13.   [*Women tendency is to love a pro-athlete for his money.* **Thus**, *women have weighed-in at 400 pounds to make love to Michael Jordan and to call me the class clown.*]

HEAVEN AND EARTH

A cloud in the sky blankets me, as I sat in my living room.
The feeling of ascending into Heaven was my expression, as I let the
feeling take over me.
I am truly at peace.
But then I received a message under my door.
The messenger left unknown.

The message stated that a significant event was about to happen.
That I needed to prepare for the inevitable because everyone in
the spiritual realm knew that I had just visit God.

So I gather my belongings and went on a journey.
Not telling a soul, I just left.
And, about three months later, the rigid frigid cold was upon my face.
I knew then that the inevitable had presented itself to my existence
and a phase of life was the message that I kept with me.

I begin to see this message as a code.
An unfolding story of life lost in which it is ascertain that humanity,
[if this is not corrected], will have to pay the cost.

It started as a simple game.
But who it was being done to did not want to play because
it would make her life the only one at stake.
So they did not ask her for her consent and now everything is ridiculous.

Men are involved in homosexual activities even though they have
wifeys.
Women are Lesbian relating even though they are married.
Children are allowed to openly consent to incest even though
it is against family planning and practice.
And all of this is happening in the United States of America but no one
lives up to it.

They want to represent this as a hidden culture.

{*First Forty*}

["VERILY I SAY UNTO YOU, THIS GENERATION [**EVERY FORTY YEARS**] SHALL NOT PASS, TILL ALL THESE THINGS BE FULFILLED" (MATTHEW 24:34).]

Therefore, I must address the inevitable now in which I know my life is of the utmost importance.
I am the leader and it is quite preposterous to deny this.

Men shall become my servants.
Not serving me but living within my identity as if they have found deliverance.
Women shall become my companions.
Not being seen with me constantly but living equitably within the world I am in.
And children shall become my mental followers.
Not following me, as if I am a leader, but giving me the philosophical role in their lives.
These images will be seen through-out humanity.

{*Last Forty*}

The message uncoded in which it told me that false leadership shall end so that man and his kind will not parish and the earth will always stand.

Heaven

14.   [*God commanded Heaven and Earth –* **STAND!** *Therefore, I have visited God in Heaven and have brought back to earth the prophecy of life forever.* **"Verily I say unto you, this generation [every forty years]** *shall not pass, till all these things be fulfilled"* **(Matthew 24:34).**

FABIEN ALAVONT BALDWIN

Loretta and Sabien Baldwin son Fabien is quite a character.
He is the image of his father and so intelligent.
However, his story isn't an easy tale to tell.
Fabien has visited Lucifer Satan's Hell.

His dreams are virtual reality.
His body is transported into surreality.
He sits at Lucifer's table to sup while Satan tells him what he will do.
The story of Fabien destiny is foretold.
However, he does not conceive what he knows.
Therefore, Fabien lives a normal human life.
Lucifer watches from his spiritual realm and when Fabien visit, he tells him over and over again.

****

My powers were given to me by God because I was in Heaven keeping up too much noise and God became angry and gave me my own personal hell and Fabien that is your dynasty as well.

*****

Fabien's eighteenth birthday came to pass, which was greatly celebrated by his mom and dad.
His other siblings celebrated Fabien's birthday as well; however, they did not know that Fabien was visiting Lucifer Satan's Hell.
Neither had Fabien shared his dreams with his dad, not once, he kept them within.
Therefore, Fabien would become a powerful man and he would be seen and heard everywhere.
Greater than the President of the United States of America or any leader of a country, Fabien had Lucifer Satan's son's identity.

Chosen by Satan himself and not by the spirit of the demonic in a jackal, Fabien was the first child of Loretta and Sabien Baldwin in which they had three (3) of each.

Thus, Fabien was metaphorically formed to be three sixes and as the first child – A true leader.

All will bow to Fabien Alavont Baldwin!

15.   **[Lucifer Satan's Hell is a spiritual place for good evil and bad evil. Have you ever visited there? If you have, make sure you do not tell and one day you may become powerful as Fabien will.]**

MARVELOUS

Obstacles, stumbling blocks, mountains to climb, bridges to cross, many
times we don't.
With God's help we focus and pray that we achieve.
Never giving up because the Lord has promised us the victory.

In God's speed is my destiny!
I must believe in a power greater than myself.
I stand on my mountains and The Word states: *"Look to the hills for*
your health!" **–**
Crossing my bridges within the Lord's intellect.

Gathering God's protective armor in which I stand for righteousness.
I project the conquering of many souls though my evangelistic journey.
All is in the name of Jehovah.

In God's speed is my spirit in which I must believe in a power
greater than my existence; kicking my stumbling blocks, as I look to
hills for my help!
Obstacles are no more and The Lord's eyesight adores, as I worship
The Almighty God.

In time, I will have acquired a Buddha presence.
And people all over the world will have seen The Almighty God – The
Lord – Jehovah.
Mankind will be more refined for the second coming of Jehovah God
Lord's son – Jesus Christ Lord - who died for all of us {*ACTS 20:21*}.
So let's join together as a universe in the magnificent.
The eyes of Jehovah God Lord is upon us and his son – Jesus Christ
Lord's – spirit is with us – knowing:

This is quite marvelous.

16. [*Life is episodic.* **Therefore**, *destiny is the dynasty partaken* **and thus**, *life is always in the making, especially when someone ordains you to fulfill a Prophecy that they foresee as a fulfillment to their fate.* "**But he** [*or she*] **that shall endure unto the end, the same shall be saved**" (Matthew 24:13).]

****

In most people lives, lives an imagination.
If one is not there, some damage has been done.
Do not believe that you have to tell anyone!

****

SABIEN ALLEGRA BALDWIN II

As the second son to the Baldwin's six, Sabien was name after his father.
He was sixteen (16) and utterly handsome.
However, Sabien had one folly, his nose.
Nevertheless, it did not take away from Sabien because he was a mystical genesis.

Sabien humor could go off the heezee.
If you got his attention with something of the non-sense, he would address you with a certain type of intelligence.
He learn this by way of his father's warlock world, which his daddy did not know he was even part of.

Sabien always appeared to his father as an animal yet, never the same one.
The last time he appeared, Sabien was a unicorn.
His father was standing near a fountain in The Garden of the Great Warlocks.

At the mere age of thirteen (13), which was three years ago, Sabien approached his father and asked: "**Have you ever talked to a unicorn**?"
His father responded and said: "**No, I don't believe I have but I have spoken with many mystical beings here**."
Thus, Sabien, as a unicorn, begin to tell his father why he was there.

*****

"The shepherd left me in the lily fields.
I was very scared.
So I ran and I am here.
I found you standing at the fountain and you seem to be so lost and
because I feel a sense of loss as well, I came to get to know who you
are."

"Well, my name is Sabien the Warlock and I am said to be great.
This is my Warlock world that I have created.
I have to be sure that all feel a sense of heaven here.
So I come periodically to make sure danger does not preservers.
And if it does, I will destroy its universe, which will become the planet
earth. Humankind will be affected because the only way danger is
present in this warlock world is by humans being aware of us through
the imagination. And therefore, they will be able to involve themselves
in this habitation. Are you aware of this unicorn?"

Sabien II did not answer.
He said: *"I have to go."*

Sabien II awoke and he knew of why his father was so
despondent when he thought no one was aware.
Why did his father reveal this to him when he was only a mystical
animal?
Sabien asked himself this question over and over again.
And, then he thought with eminent intelligence: *"Could father know it*
was him? His son Sabien!"
Sabien knew he would never divulge this to The Distinguished
One who had let him into his father's warlock world.
Nonetheless, he almost told his father about the Distinguished one.

Inasmuch, this begins the divine providence of *Sabien the Mystical*.

17. *[Sabien Allegra Baldwin II is his father's son and shall*
become mystical – a great one].

Today was an exceptional day in History.
Many things came to pass when I spread my legs.
But I still live in yesterday because men are waiting for the same damn thing to transgress.

****

SEX

Sexual intercourse is unheard of in the world I live in.
Men want to suppress me for saying sex over and over again.
No meaning in the word at all but just a word to say when you don't know what is wished for.
So sex it is girls and boys.

Why didn't you simply ask for what you lack?
You took it to highest to try take my life.
But man only I can live my destiny and therefore, you will continue to aspire to kill me.

Sex is a mental dominant factor.
If you desire me, than you will keep coming after me.
However, what if I don't desire you?
Then you ascertain to lose!

You could have put it in simple terms.
You could have plainly stated what you wanted.
But you wanted to play mind games instead.
Now, man who is plunked into insanity?
Don't look at me.
I'm not your identity.
I only said sex.
Why did you do something with that?
Once again – *SEX*!
Remember, it is only a word.

18.   *[I merely said sex and men who put me in mind sets and outer body experience fucked everything in The United States of America –The USA. Can you believe that? If you don't or if you do, just say sex! They will fuck you as well!]*

****

When I come home, I like to relax.

Then I encounter male anxiety attacks.

They begin to lose their minds over my unwinding.

****

THE STORY OF THE HAILEY BROTHERS

Looking out my living room window, I see William Hailey.
He is my neighbor from upstairs.
I live in a two family flat in Detroit, Michigan and he asserts the
deportment toward me as a nemesis.

He suggests that he has the power of the demonic.
His brother Lawrence Hailey standpoint is he is done because
he started this first and then left by moving in with his girlfriend
on 8th mile and Dequindre.
However, it makes one begin to wonder what is wrong with
these hot boys – **The Hailey Brothers**.

Therefore, I will begin to discuss what Lawrence did first.

I moved into this flat in October 2009 and as I was sitting in the
car with my landlord, Paula Dixon, when Lawrence Hailey
came and spoke to her because he was her tenant also.
Simultaneously, he spoke to me as well while holding my hand
intimately, as if he had met me somewhere else.

As time pass, Lawrence, whose nickname is Rokie, begin to do
extrasensory things toward my person, which trigger my
telekinetic domain.
He would make loud noises upstairs and his brother Will would
act as if he was not a part of what Lawrence did.
However, he was because after Lawrence left Will states he
will complete it.
He will finish what was not finished.

In the meantime, someone damage my tag and Lawrence came to my door and told me that in which Lawrence knew who did this because all on this block was discussing it, as if I should let them have my car next.
Do you think I'll be consensual to this just to get along with everyone in this vicinity?
Not in a million years and that is what for real is!

Now let me tell you about Will.

Will was sitting on the porch one day.
He's a drug dealer by the way.
He had his weed bags selling them.
Apparently he thinks he can do this through my life.
How is this so when I am not even Will's wife?

Because of the conspiracy in my existence and how I conspire to ensure they cannot take my normal world, Will believes that I am his protection.
So he openly sells drugs without hesitation or procrastination, as if he is above the law and in Detroit, a City of corruption, who knows Will connection with Law Enforcement.

Thus, as long as I live at 4714 Saint Clair Street in Detroit, Michigan, **The Story of the Hailey Brothers** will continue.

Oh, and, by the way, Will roommate now is his friend.
Paula told me his name but I can't remember it and he wants to be my fate as well.
He does things silently and then smiles at me, as if he is winning when only he is lost because his detriment is Will and how they live!
Therefore, when Tinkerbelle comes and ask: "**Did she do you Will**?"
I am here watching her destroy herself as female.

But that is the same story but not directly here where I live. This is just a person that lives in the same neighborhood stating she has hood love.

Hence, Divine Providence will prevail and destiny is handcuffs and shackles to those who are against Poethics!

19. **[To understand why the bottom is at the bottom is to understand why poverty exists. To understand why a poor man or woman is in existence is to be understood as the complexity of the world. When all this understanding is within society, then poverty is a detrimental factor faithfully forever.]**

HARDIK SHAH

Today he was with me - informing *Poethics* that he really fit
into her fantasy.
He stated: "**We will study manipulate.
I am not a fetish because your heart is at stake.**"

He's not going to reject me after all.
He wants to be very close.
Hardik Shah is his name.
He is my doctor but also desires to be my man.

He talks to Jamie about the treatment she is taking.
He asked her did she feel it was working.
She states that she was in so much pain that she was really
trying to stay focus.
All this basal conversation going on while he did my
adjustments and all I was thinking about is whether or not I
could seduce him.

Hardik Shah is so exciting.
He really thrills me.
A beautiful man stands before me, which is passion to deep for
psychology.

Hardik, I ask of you fulfillment.
My body is aching to know yours though a medium that only
you and I know of.
We should be able to keep the world out, as we reveal our
treasures.

Both of us are the same and my name is *Poethics Oblivion
Stareyes*.

Hardik, I will achieve this for you and I.

20.   *[Poethics and Hardik, a romance that is truly an epic.]*

BRITTANY & FELIX BALDWIN

In the womb they fought for whom would come first and
Loretta Baldwin knew it.
She quietly talked to her husband Sabien so that he knew what
to expect.
Fraternal twins would come next.
****

Brittany was the first.
Felix was second.
Girl and boy, fraternal twins they were.
Fourth and fifth child of the Baldwin's six and what powers
they represent.
In Brittany's world was no pretense.
She knew everything about human.
But unlike one of her siblings before her, she would not be
medicinal but ascertain to the philosophical world.
Her powers were those of a Goddess.
She could caste spells and could change a person identity.
And if and when this was done, nothing could be done about it.
She was not even considered to be a witch.
Brittany took her mother's reddish blonde hair, her father's
beautiful smile, and as all the Baldwin's children, a persona that
was streamlined.
And as her mind developed, her philosophical role in this world
would be established.
Loretta had already written books with her daughter and now
she was only ten years old and was branching out as an author
of philosophy on her own.
She would use a pseudonym to be sought until she became of
age and then she would remove this disguise and come alive as
Brittany Maria Baldwin.

Felix came second and he did not take kindly of it.

He was mad because during the last trimester Brittany was given preference by God because of her weak heart.
Loretta and Sabien did not know this because Felix promise God he would kept it sacred and therefore, Brittany would never suffer from any heart condition as long as Felix control his temper and did not mention this when Brittany poked fun about him being second.
Both were ten now and Brittany, for whatever may be, had never poked fun at Felix about him being the second fiddler.

Felix powers were that of a God and he was superb in any sport.
Felix destiny showed his Father that he would not become a Master Warlock like his other two sons but skilled in archery, heavy artillery, a brilliant strategic war man never to fight in any military but that of Jehovah God Lord's, which he would because Felix had be chosen by God to be an immortal and therefore, he would not be ascertain to his father's, Sabien, Warlock World.

Felix & Brittany Baldwin are now ten.
They are within the world of man but also know of their godly realm.
They are fraternal twins but very close.
They know what no other knows.
But what is so mystical and powerful about each is they met during procreation and knew that they were to be fraternal twins.
Felix closes his eyes and states my mother will name me Felix Lalegra Baldwin and Loretta did.

From one end of Heaven to the other.
From the four winds of Jehovah Lord, The Almighty God, stands Earth and its habitants.
Not perfect to what they see or perceive only flawed and mislead because they believe in what they say – in what has been said!

****

LORETTA LULA PRISTINE-BALDWIN

Many desired Loretta Lula Pristine but she had eyes for only Sabien Allegra Baldwin.
Through telepathic means, she connected to his warlock realm in the form of a dove.
Her gift had been passed down through traditional measures, only this tradition was pure to sacred and no one knew who had blessed the Pristine family but God.

However, one day a sparrow came to Loretta's window and told her the story of telekinetic and prophecy.
Not even knowing Sabien at that particular moment, she was teleported into a vision and her entire family came along.
Let it be known that Loretta Lula Pristine was only thirteen (13) years old.

"This world I am in" thought Loretta, **"seems to be unreal."**
A magical place in which I have made friends and one that draws my attention the most is this boy name Sabien.
The sparrow told me that I would fall in love young and the male of my choice would have supernatural powers.
He said telekinetic was the prophecy I lived in and: *"Know Loretta that you will be desired by woman and man!*
Nevertheless, *don't be afraid.*
Loretta, you will know what to do when the time gets here."

The sparrow disappear but would visit Loretta throughout the years.

Sabien knew Loretta also.
They would go to the same attendance center.
He would become the Valedictorian and Loretta would be the Salutatorian of their class, however, Loretta would be two (2) years younger.
And then tragedy would happen.

****

Mayhem in the world we live in and all standing are blessed people who will discover why they are so set apart from the lucky ones.
Jehovah God Lord through his son Jesus Christ Lord developed a plan, which implementation is embedded.
Yet and still in The City of Exalt, Loretta and Sabien are Warlocks.
Powers given to them in Divine Providence and must be combined through marriage so that all may be exalted and accepted by the Warlock World.
A World created by the presence of the spirit of Jehovah God Lord and his son – Jesus Christ Lord – our salvation and purgatory into the Heaven above.

****

Their meeting was evident to their schooling at the Attendance Center.
Loretta was on all the clubs Sabien was on, except the ones that where male oriented.
Sabien was on all the clubs Loretta was on, except the ones that where female oriented.
This is what would bring them together in holy matrimony.

The timing was right and this would fulfill the world's divination in which the day of judgment was only known by Sabien.

Loretta knew when the last days were upon us in which this would be true prediction.

Being husband and wife, foresight was foretelling through perils and through the birth of Loretta Lula and Sabien Allegra Baldwin's children, who was mention earlier.

Both first origins were from the Continent Asia.

Iran – Loretta and Iraq – Sabien with first origin surnames being Nurinamedinorhide [Loretta Lula] (Iranian) and Abdulzahara-Hussein [Sabien Allegra]

(Iraqi) in which Loretta was from a fourth (4th) generation Iranian family and

Sabien was from a third (3rd) generation Iraqi family in the United States of America.

This was rarity at that time in America's [U.S.] Immigration History.

Therefore, the premonition is such a metamorphosis that the United States of America [U.S.A.] Immigration History can change the stance of Independence in the U.S.A.

Right today, which is July 09, 2010, Iran is in a Revolution and Loretta knows the prediction of the Last Days and when they shall be upon the universe.

Sabien, which is Loretta's husband, is the world's divination and the day of judgment is known only by the created origin of Abdulzahra-Hussein and Sabien is the last of this surname.

Loretta is visionary and Sabien knows the universe vision and its godly mission.

Change will come and it is not foreseen as white Hispanic but transformation through transmutation via procreation.

Those that are White Americans shall mate with neutralized Americans and Hispanic shall be just a decimal in the population of interracial and the rest of the motif shall become tinted as well.

Meaning being, white superiority shall not prevail.

21. [**Today's date is July 9, 2010 and Afghanistan has decapitated the United States of America soldiers in whole via the platoons we deploy and they then destroy the entire unit in the war against terrorism leaving not one soldier alive. Well we ever claim the victory through how many from each country has died?** *Matthew 24:2 {New International Version} – "I tell you the truth, not one stone here will be left on another; everyone will be thrown down."*]

HARMONICA

In the destiny of all is a vision foretold.
In that vision is a trial and a purpose.
Only the holy knows if the crossing is safe.
Light of the day is as dark as the night, if that is what you have
to face.

****

I am what many say I should not be.
And that is an angel within humanity.
I am the third child of the Baldwin's six.
My mother love's me senseless.
My father tries to not dote as much but he knows as well that I
am chosen by God.
They name me Harmonica because I harmonize when there are
problems.
Many do not even know I have done such, being that I am only
twelve years old.

I know about my father's warlock world.
It is a part of God's Divine Order.
My brother Fabien is supposed to be chosen by Lucifer but that
is only God in reverse.
Do you know what I mean by that?
Well Lucifer Satan is the Angel God banish from Heaven.
However, God's Angels are infinity throughout eternity.
This means God controls Satan's equity and identity.
Therefore, my brother Fabien will be as his Father is a Master
Warlock and Lucifer will always be Satan.

Now let me tell a little about myself.
In destiny I will achieve the presence of a Physician.

I will find the cure for some dreaded disease and become renown.

But my prominence will be with Jehovah God Lord and I will speak to him via the mind.

As I become older, I will gain distinction in the neurological world as a top doctor.

So great I am that when I do marry, this man will not be able to be my soul mate.

I will go to my father and mother for advice and they will tell me to talk to God Lord Jehovah.

Within a dream, I will visit The Lord and ask for guidance.

As I ascend, there stand my husband, mother, and father.

Little did I know that this man was chosen for me when I was merely a toddler.

Therefore, as The Lord spoke, I touched my father's cloak and watched my mother smile and my husband told me he was God.

That is just a glimpse in my destiny.

In closure, I will leave you with my complete identity, which is Harmonica Deontia Baldwin.

In the mist of another world is a labyrinth. Epic to the time it is within and that is forever and another world relived again with no ending to hypocrisy and gnashing of teeth. This world can cut you to pieces.

{*************************}

QUEASY QUEEN KINGDOM PARADISE (THE MOVIE VERSION)

(CHAPTER I)

Quite ashamed was Queasy Queen. As her stomach swells, she paints her nails. Her hair hangs long, as she props her feet while taking a tooth pick through her teeth. Rising, her stomach returns to normal size. Queasy Queen blinks her eyes. Quiet, quite she says to the maggots. Quiet, quiet she says to the flies. The bumble bees buzz and in her ears they fly with a hermaphrodite life composing Queasy Queen hair into a Beehive.

The maggots stood still. The flies are at ease. This is Queasy Queen's family. All she has. As the ants begins to laugh, Queasy, the insectimologist stands and defines her career. Swinging her feet from a branch of a morsella tree, a recluse is her captivity. She has lived for the last hundreds of years, Rumplestilskin with whoop-a-peal. Neither man nor woman, how does she exist? A maze and not amazing is her subsistence because no man knows of her way of life. Fatherless is Queasy's reality and if man capture this knowledge, him and his kind will envy this through-out mentality.

Queasy is beautiful. She is magnetic. She is truly a creature of the earth in which she magnificently transforms into anything she wishes. Fortunate Queasy is. Transgression of three (3) thousand centuries in this millennium of disbelief because once her kingdom is discovered (if ever), she will be what she is with no further explanation to give. Man and his kind must accept her as a future deliverance. Immorality will be before them. There tomorrows will become enriched - making the Biblical years high Imagination and a symbolic myth. Queasy Queen will dignify life and make believe will be done so that mortality and immorality can live as one. Honorability and from a land of nowhere well be how Queasy will spin her wand. Thus, her introduction into humanity will be embodied, however, never encapsulated by anyone.

****

Queasy Queen is the Queen of her paradise. A Queen domed of such difference that her paradise is full of maladaptation, which are abnormalities that procreate normally. No man or his kind on Planet Earth knows of this Kingdom Paradise. However, it is attached to Planet Earth but is detached from man's knowledge. Queasy sees many Things and Beings – even this...

BIG BIRD TRILOGY AND PSYCHOLOGY

A man and his son was traveling a journey afar when they saw how to invent surreal life forms, which are things that are not are. To get him a sexual fix the father invented himself a yogavig so him and his son could perform incest. His son was name Bone who he began to dike. Though the yogavig the father and son changed into birds for mating purposes. And, once this mating was completed, the father gave birth to another baby as a dropping.

Since the father was a doctor, who in Kingdom Paradise was of little importance, the son made more money as an inventor. The father and son fell in love at first sight. They were beings made by Queasy Queen during a special night of the opening of her Kingdom Paradise. At first the father called himself **"Build the Ocean"** but change his name to Big Bird. His son was a comedian at first but change his name to Bone the Inventor.

Now the son feels at lost knowing his father must die. Not trying to hurt but the truth has to be told to his dad. Mocking birds do fly. Laughing so hard, tears began to roll from Bone's eyes because he is the son and his father is the old man but Bone holds all the wisdom.

The baby bird has grown within Queasy Queen Kingdom Paradise. She denies the revelation, which gives true freedom to Big Bird, Bone, and Tree Frog, which is the baby bird name. How many times do we forget the value of life? In a minute, we must wait and began to think before we leap and decide to procreate. Queasy Queen has gotten the word about the coming of Tree Frog and her judgment will be done in the morning. Therefore, as night falls, we light the house and remember that Queasy judges all.

[*Morning comes*] QUEASY QUEEN SPEAKS…*"Be faithful to your Tree Frog, your Daddy, and your Big Bird!"*

(Chapter II)

BONE, BEAN POLE, AND TREE FROG

A description of three –

Have you ever seen a hollow tree that has a hole in the center? It's gotten rotten and its branches are brittle. A storm comes in mid-May and makes the tree into a stump and in momentary insanity out jumps Bone in the tree form. So hollow, he is clearly transparent.

The skin on the bones sticks while the eyes protrude and the mouth shows teeth constantly, standing, leaning, bending down is a pole. A frame of a body with arms stretched from here to yonder, walk Bean Pole.

In a dream, maybe a nightmare, a man that I know was running back and forth. He is as tall as the eyes can see. His nose grows in front of me. Clothes mean not anything to this man. As long as he is as tall as his nose, which is this man sadness because it tells all that he has been damned by fools. His name is Tree Frog.

****

Queasy Queen Kingdom Paradise has many Beings. Bone, Bean Pole, and Tree Frog are Beings and live there. Not even knowing what family is, the threesome are as close as family can be. They live in close proximity doing what well. One morning in Early Suntex, Bone, Bean Pole, and Tree Frog joined together to travel to a certain destination, which would be a journey that was dangerous as well as mysterious. They set out to find their blessings. Bone is the soldier of inventions. Bean Pole is the foe of their enemies. And, Tree Frog will know that these two will betray him in some way or another. Tree Frog is the true brother to all but have no true brothers of his own. He sits out to make everyone in Kingdom Paradise more than he, except one person that shows him what he is worth – not spit from snuff that comes out the mouth.

There is a ridiculous Being that is involved. He has gold teeth from mineral ores in his jaws. He is as ugly as ugly can be. He wants everyone in Kingdom Paradise to see '**me**.' That's another tale altogether, however, it goes with Tree Frog because this is his exceptional one.

Queasy Queen knows all that lives in her Kingdom Paradise. Bone, Bean Pole, and Tree Frog gives her misgivings since they are about to set out on a journey without her blessings.

++++++++++++++++++++

Darkness of night – Brightness of day - The men that travel know their way. Caste a shadow of darkness in their days. Caste a shadow of brightness in their nights. When their journey is done, turn the lights out making sure they are unfortunate. Their blessings never to be claim. They cannot get away with this. Authority has not been given by me for them to travel on this destiny. Therefore, they have issues in which you will bring them back to Kingdom Paradise because without light they will surely die. They will know that the signs of darkness have been met. Mediocre as it may seem, they will never fulfill their dreams for violating the policy and/or protocol of Kingdom Paradise, which is owned and ruled by Queasy Queen.

BEAN POLE: I am not tired. We know what we are looking for.

BONE: I'm stone, not tired, and just high because stupidity stands in front of me: the desert that we must and will cross easily. Many say that desert is perilous for any Being to walk. We know differently. This desert is nothing to you, you, and me.

TREE FROG: I want to go home. I know I want to go home.

$$* *$$

During the final day of the journey, casting begins; however, Queasy Queen wishes are not fulfilled. Casting shadows of darkness in days and shadows of brightness in nights caused changes in Bone, Bean Pole, and Tree Frog Beings into beautiful Human Beings. Amazing as it may be, Queasy Queen had given her Beings destiny. They became part of Planet Earth that exist. No longer living in suspended time but refined to real life. Queasy Queen did know this was a possibility but she disregarded the knowledge because if it truly happened, Queasy knew she planned this in which the Super Natural Realm controlled Happenings. Bone, Bean Pole, and Tree Frog never would become rich, which Queasy Queen subconsciously had deemed, if and when destiny happened to one of her Things or Beings, this would be called desperturent.

Totally oblivious to where they were from, Bone, Bean Pole, and Tree Frog lived as humans. As Queasy Queen look on watching Bone, Bean Pole, and Tree Frog with their families on Planet Earth, will the threesome ever remember Yester Year and will Queasy Queen release them from their dreams of richness so that they may acquire wealth abundantly?

PIER, TIER, AND, LEDGE

Pier and pyemia are synonymous. Tier and rotten teeth lack anonymity. Ledge and gas are watching me. But what is definite is their jealousy. Therefore, Queasy Queen will create false imagery.

Queasy Queen has many Things and Beings in her Kingdom Paradise. She places her crystal ball on earth. She sees Pier, Tier, and

Ledge who lives as Humans but who are just Beings and Things. As their lives unfold, will they ever be told?

***

****

Pier is very excited about her discovery. She knows her destiny. At least this is what she believes. She doesn't know anything about deceit, therefore, she continues to believe that she has a destiny. As she looks for her soul mate, she knows she is just like everyone else. Thus, her physiology and anatomy are the same as humans, however, she lacks true identity because she does not know what nationality is only what she learned in school. For that reason, when she made friends in school, her blood mutated giving her certain supernatural powers that she evaded.

Tier is Pier next-door neighbor on Planet Earth. Tier has a description of a child with a birth defect. He walks with a brace on his left leg. In Queasy Queen Kingdom Paradise this would be called "**monique**" meaning a supernatural being.

Ledge visits every Summer [Suntex in Queasy Queen Kingdom Paradise] with her earthly parents to see her grandparents in the city Tier and Pier lives in, which is called Dogpit, Kansas . She is quite adorable and poetic in a certain sense, however, never to make sense.

****

Queasy Queen changes into a visitor of all families of Pier, Tier, and Ledge. This is what she did.

****

QUEASY QUEEN SPEAKING!

Kingdom Paradise open your mouth and let me out. I must go to the Planet Mother Earth, which is not of us but attached to us to bring my three Beings back. One is not seen as just right but that he is alright. One is seen to be intact but not worthy of that. Last would be just like Queasy Queen – quite adorable. The mortals will destroy who they are for sure. I must return them to Kingdom Paradise this very night.

****

The wings of my stalk spread wide! The darkness of my bat blind eyes! Transcend in a landing in the woods nearby! As I silently rescue Pier, Tier, and Ledge before Human eyes, we'll caste a spell so they will not remember anything. The Humans will believe they have been dreaming.

****

ESPIONAGE:

Smoke from the stalk

Darkness from the bat coloration

Caste the spell

Espionage – A success!

Pier, Tier, and Ledge was given an identity that lacks a fate because now they live in immortality. Queasy Queen has claimed another victory but there is the question of Bone, Bean Pole, and Tree Frog. Are they forever in destiny?

TO DO ONE IS TO DO ALL

Queasy Queen is the leader in this cause. Kingdom Paradise she mandates and controls. Queasy Queen knows that immortality has no age. Days become years quickly. Queasy Queen is eon and eternity.

****

Music of the maggots, lyrics of the flies, ants prancing, and all the insects and worms began choreographing in a dance mapping out a plan. Queasy Queen takes a stance on her peak [seeing all including me]. "Who you will be," she asked. My response was, "I'll Get The Last Laugh." "What does that mean," she asked. "I asked you your name." "My name is: "I'll Get The Last Laugh." I responded. [Queasy Queen speaking] "But that is not a name. That's a phrase. You are from my

Kingdom Paradise. I can tell. Who your family will be?" [I'll Get the Last Laugh Speaking] "No one but me!" [Queasy Queen Speaking] "Will since I am your Superior, your name is and has always been Jim. Spread the word about your identity."

The festivity continues. Kingdom Paradise has no recourse in their rejoicing!

Darkness transcends – Night transgresses – Queasy Queen says, "Leave the mess!"

Laughing hastily, Queasy Queen speaks: "Shit in the corner – Male Maggot's sumteat! In the morning, Kingdom Paradise will be as clean as clean can be."

JIM

The diamond head of a cubic stone, the goldenness and the crown, smiles a jolly man, young or old is not known, which spread messages, news, and **The Word of Queasy Queen** to all who goes in Kingdom Paradise. How not amazing this may seem! Why does it seem like that? In a Biblical sense, God did the same thing. Only Jim is not Queasy Queen offspring. But do we really know this. Although Jim story remains untold, until now, Jim says he has no family but he truly exist as an immortal in Queasy Queen Kingdom Paradise.

****

Waking early one morning in immortality, I knew my name to be Jim. And, as life progress I began to laugh senseless. Mind and body all as one, however, did I lack a soul? Nevertheless, my story must be told but do I know it?

****

I met maggots and flies on my fifth day and the ants lead the way. We built my meager homage from the lumber the trees gave. All my provisions were made, um, someway. I knew Queasy Queen but hadn't met her yet until Festivity. She knew my name and told me. My head contains carotene that gives light and glows with all Things and Beings. Never tell you have seen me.

****

QUEASY QUEEN DIVINITY

If you are not cautious, you over protect. If you are not curious, you over neglect. Is the Thing and Being that truly knows his or her way! Queasy Queen Words I say. This book will be open again another day with **The Words of Queasy Queen** from Jim.

(Chapter III)

QUEASY QUEEN CONTINUES:

If this is my Kingdom Paradise, this is my pilgrimage. This is my immortality. This is my lifelessness. Destiny belongs to me. Identity I give. All are immortals. Man cannot live here. No man knows of us. We are attach but detached from human reality. Things and Beings stand to get recognize.

CHANTING!

Kingdom, Kingdom Paradise open your mouth and let Things and Beings out. Kingdom Paradise we hear you as you speak. Kingdom Paradise is where we live. Mankind will continue to adhere to their ignorance. Marvels, magical, mystical, to magnificent stands the Throness. Authority of Things and Beings, Queasy Queen is majestic honoring all the Stars while the Moon bows. Suntex stands in unison praising our Queasy Queen. This is her Kingdom Paradise of all Things and Beings. Give praise, respect, and adherence or The Supernatural Realm will kick your ass. Do you hear us!

****

Ass is crystal clear here. It protrudes and will smell if you do not take care of yourself. It could be flat but still will stink when you forget to wash it. Queasy Queen makes, takes, and caste and because of this Things and Beings meek any creature that thinks he can dethrone Queasy Queen. Please make note of that and better yet, take it as an antidote for your knowledge.

UNKEMPT DERANGED

A place in time with a rhyme in place, Tells of many endless nights that man will live. A blessing of stupidity that utilizes his dick for everything in life, even, he says to cure those that are in [S]undry, which is in difference from other Things and Beings!

*********************   **********************

Queasy Queen Kingdom Paradise has many Things and Beings. Unkempt was born deranged and plus that is his surname. However, in Kingdom Paradise he is seen as a marvel. The oldest of the immortals he makes love to. He desires the wisdom and knowledge of Kingdom Paradise. His plot is to dethrone Queasy Queen forever and become the King of Kingdom Paradise.

**********************   ************************

Unkempt Deranged identity is known by all in Kingdom Paradise. He is seen as highly intelligent. Things and Beings have said his mind is more powerful than Queasy Queen. This is how he is seen. He has a very small nose with big teeth. Ears that are mice size with a head that can expand the universe but is normal size around us – Things and Beings. His anatomy is that of a porcupine with neck, shoulder, arms, stomach, hips, legs, and feet of a man; however, skin porcupines when he gets mad. Queasy Queen let all know that this is her enmity. Does Unkempt cares? Why of course not! Here is an introduction of Unkempt. Don't go derange!

**********************   ************************

I AM UNKEMPT DERANGED!
I HAVE A FIRST AND LAST NAME.
I AM FROM THIS KINGDOM PARADISE.
SILENCE! JUST BE QUIET.
WHERE ARE ALL MY FOLLOWERS?

THE MAGGOTS, THE FLIES, AND THE ANTS ROARED. SAYING AND ASKING UNKEMPT: "WHAT IS OUR DESTINY?"

[UNKEMPT SPEAKING] "I IDENTIFIED QUEASY QUEEN IN THE TREES. SHE LISTENS BUT SHE DOES NOT HEAR ME. SHE WONDERS WHY SHE DOES NOT HEAR ME. WE ALL KNOW. NOW LET US SHOW HER THE WAY TO GO!"

WHAT UNKEMPT DERANGED DID NOT KNOW WAS THAT THE SUPERNATURAL REALM HEARD HIM. SO HE CASTE A SPELL ON KINGDOM PARADISE. TO SHORTEN THE TALE IT WAS NOT NICE. EVERY THING AND BEING IN KINGDOM PARADISE SLEPT FOR TEN YEARS. EVEN QUEASY QUEEN SEEM TO BE ILL. UNKEMPT MADE KINGDOM PARADISE AMBIENT SURROUNDING - 'HEAVENLY'- CHANGING ITS APPPEARANCE INTO A MORTALITY DESTINY.

SUPERNATURAL REALM AWAKEN ME!
I FEEL AS IF I HAVE BEEN SLEEPING FOR A MILLION YEARS. I AM QUEASY QUEEN! YOUR DOMINION RULINGS ARE TO PROTECT ME. I KNOW MY KINGDOM PARADISE HAS BEEN MADE "HEAVENLY." I KNOW NOT WHAT ALIENATES ME. UNKEMPT DERANGED IS MY KINGDOM ENMITY? HE IS THE ONE WHO MADE KINGDOM PARADISE "HEAVENLY?"

AS THE SUPERNATURAL REALM LISTENS, ENTITY SPEAKS: "ENTITY HEARD OF YOUR BLESSINGS, HOWEVER, THIS IS NOT OF UNKEMPT DERANGED MAKING. THIS IS HIS MISTAKE. UNKEMPT

DERANGED KNEW NOT WHAT WAS AT STAKE! FOREWARN IS FORESEEN IN KINGDOM PARADISE. UNKEMPT WILL NOT BE PUNISHED. HE HAS NOT HURT ANYONE. HE HAS ONLY PUT ALL OF KINGDOM PARADISE TO SLEEP INCLUDING YOU, QUEASY QUEEN.

WAKEN WAKEN KINGDOM PARADISE SO [YOUR] QUEASY QUEEN CAN GET BETTER. SHE'S ILL BECAUSE YOU SLEEP. THINGS AND BEINGS MUST HELP BECAUSE YOU CAN MAKE A DIFFERENCE, AS DID UNKEMPT. YOUR KINGDOM PARADISE UNKEMPT HAS MADE BEAUTIFUL. AS QUEASY QUEEN SAYS, "HEAVENLY!" NOW LIVE MORE ABUNDANTLY."

THE SPELL IS LIFTED. NOT EVEN QUEASY QUEEN NOR UNKEMPT KNOWS OF THIS!

[NOT COMPLETED!]

THIS SECTION IS ON DOMESTIC VIOLENCE!

In Essence

I dream of lovers' passion.
A life that has by pass me
But love has always been on the horizon.
So fragile it did not last.
As time would have it, I would never find the right man.

The ending of a dynasty is not an ending of a destiny.
Love is meant to be and passion is still foreseen.
In essence, the man of my dreams may be within me.

THEREFORE,

Conceptual to me is beauty and the beast.
Desire of imagery is a mental scene.
Reality will become an episodic existence.
I decipher my love being passionately fulfilled.
Many horizons I could acquire with the right man beside me.

WHEREFORE,

In a trance I am and the man is now holding me tightly and
God knows this is pure excitement!

If I am to win this dream of lovers' passion, my destiny will
become my dynasty.
Horizons acquired throughout life though the imagery held
within my eyes.

MORE SO,

This is because the right man is the one within and not a
dream denied.

When you say you hate me, do you mean it?
When you say you love me, what is the meaning of that?
We incompatible and that's the way it is!

Do I ask too much of you?
Is that why we cannot soul mate?
If so, then you really hate me!

Disappear out my life.
Walk away!
Don't look back.
And, then I will soon be out of your mind.

What is it you lack now?
Why have you not left my house?
I know.
I will just put your ass out!

Vanish! Kaboom!
Finally, that bitch is gone.
Magical powers I do have.
It did not take long when I told him his ass was out here.
And, now a new man is in.
So happens it's my X's best friend.

Y'ALL CAN'T STAND ME!

SECTION ON DOMESTIC VIOLENCE

When I begin to think about what I want to say I just wait to
appropriate time and state the situation to my mate.
He does not seem to respect that I need my personal space.
So I begin to separate from his environment and that is when
he becomes ballistic.

Being Indian-Negro, my blood boils warm and not cold.
I need my own personal oval to find myself but when I tell
my mate that he becomes airborne.
So I begin to contemplate whether this relationship is a
mistake and do I really consider this as a happy home.

Possessively, he characterizes us as soul mates.
Obsessively, he wants to control me.
But, I will not just be his doormat and let him do me like that.
So I begin to deliberate and as I problem solve, he will enter
the room desiring involvement.
Going ballistic is not the thing.
I am a woman who needs to be spiritually free.

This section is on domestic violence and the ideal is to talk
about it.
So as I critical think, I must write poetry.
This assists me in knowing is this man right for me but he
hates this embedded characteristic and because of it he wants
to become domestic violent.

Finding at last my personal oval, I do not shut him out.
However, he is like a propeller in motion and he does not
want me out his sight when we are together
and that is the majority of the time and when we are not, he is
constantly on the phone line.
Meaning, he goes ballistic in which he becomes extremely

angry and that is when he threatens to beat me.

He never does.
He calms down and show me tell me he loves me.
Basically, what does this means?
Well, do I know he will not hit me?
When he does I must leave and not become another violated
scene.

Domestic violence comes in many forms.
My mate is destructive but this does not cause me any harm.
The question becomes: *Am I safe from injury*?
In the event he is ever around me when he has his temper
tantrums, an injury is forthcoming.

Therefore, I will not become a victim of domestic violence.

Ms. Sweet Talks

Mary V. states that she provokes her man to keep him.
If he cannot let his emotions out, he will surely leave her.

Velma Lee says she knows how to keep a man.
She just let him know that he's in command.

Mary V. and Velma Lee are sisters but not twins and both
instructs on how to hold on to your mate.
Both are different but they become the same.

Rosie Mae is deceased. Therefore, she will not be a part of
this poetry piece.

Verlena just listens in and knows that she always will be
ahead of her man.
However, he will be in charge as well through how he treats
her in bed.

Verlena, Mary V., and Velma Lee are all sisters.
Carrie Mae Sexton daughters.
Rosie Mae is deceased who was the oldest of the three.

In Leland, these girls were true leaders in the game of love.
Therefore, they should be adulation.

This is not intended as an insult and please do not mistaken it
for –

Sycophancy!

DR. ALATASSI

I usually don't tell a lie.
I'll tell you what is truly happening.
If you felt I did, then you will inquire because I see you
Alatassi in my mind's eye.

I'm usually very truthful so in the event you question my
honesty that is telling me of my mind setting.
Am I a psychological world or a psychiatric performance?
When answering this question, remember I am not your
woman.

Evil lurks where I seem to roam, even when I am safe at
home.
Although I state we are not mates, do you feel this way?
Reason has it to be that you know what is best for me.
I must say I will try your way to see how long it takes for me
to know that I have made a mistake in not following your
instructions sooner than I did yesterday.

Alatassi, don't be afraid.
I will not provoke or incite your evil ways.
I do not want you to be angry because this may cause further
conflict in which I do not want to become your outlet.

When I do visit you again, within three months is the plan.
I will be sure to have done as you have said at night when I
go to bed.
And then when you have read my thoughts and check them
all out, we will not be at the same end and as you said, we
will go from there and Alatassi, you win.

A STORY IN HISTORY

He asked: "*Why do you do 'us'?*"
I responded by asking: "*Why should I not? You are not trying
to do me?*"
He became unresponsive and rose to leave.

****

This body of mine causes a man's mind to want to be
abusive.
He wants to hit me because I know how to use it.
So our involvement has been lessened by me to insure that he
does not feel a sense of unity.
This really is not a long-term relationship.
He's just here in a sexual partnership and therefore, harmony
is only in the bed.
He must know that this is the way it is.

He screams at me because I am not at a milieu on time.
I tell him I am not really his woman and he must have lost his
mind.
He states, however, that I am his sex partner and he does not
like to wait.
I smile and said: "**I am not really that late.**"
This is done because of the love we are about to make.
So I show teeth that way it well be great!

He yells when we climax.
I asked: "**Now are you happy?**"
He stated: "**As long as you promise not to be late from
here on.**"
My response was: "**You know I cannot promise that but
I'll do my best to pass your test.**"
We hugged and I left.

Several more occasions past and he began to be oppressive
because now he wanted to be my only man.
He had agreed to this open relationship at the start.
Promptly, he states he wants to be my only choice.
At this point, I do not want to be involved with only one man
holding onto my arm.
Therefore, I told him no and he became irate and lets me
know that I have just made a mistake in which he hits me in
the face.
Enraged, I deliver my blow, which folded him and he became
more infuriated.
A domestic violent scene I had created and this man was
incensed by me defending self, thus, believing I belonged
only to him.

Finally, this abuse end and I leave never to be with this man
in life again.

UPSHOT

I am not going to be your damn fool.
I may love you unconditionally but I refused to be used.
You're abusive and that is no lie.
I have seen many blacken eyes.
In this home of mine, I am the breadwinner.
You are just a damn drug dealer.

This is not an actual occurrence but a tale that needs to be
told.
He may seem to be a very sweet person but he is only a life
unfolding.
You are not going to push me around as if I am your
cannabis, bitch you are going to be between my legs as if you
are cannibalistic.

I am not going to be foolish for you.
And, if you don't believe me, continue to try me with the
things you do.
I am trying to understand and that's why I am
confrontational.
However, when I asked you did you lie about what you lied
about you still do not tell me the truth.

This is an actual occurrence.
A tale that has been told so many times and what is so sad
about it, the man continues to lie.

I am not your punching bag nor are we in a boxing ring.
So why do I constantly have to deal with you in a domestic
violent scene?
Just metaphoric terms I am stating here because this
relationship I am escaping my dear.

In the event that you come looking for me, you may find the closer of your destiny.

I refuse to be used and abused.

EXTREMITIES STRETCHED

Termination of a relationship can cause stress when the man
does not want to leave.
In reality, you must leave and then, a scene can manifest.

****

What caused the strike?
Why did you try to take my life?
You said it was over Honey Boo.
So I decided to leave to.
Why did you come looking for me?
You found me with my new man.
Told me I had him while I was with you.
But that is so untrue.
I never keep a spare tire.
Men just come when others leave my life.

The closing stages of our relationship states that you were
cheating and not me and therefore, I felt I needed to leave.
Now here you come with this domestic violent scene and I
don't even care what this means.
I called the police and they did not do anything [**as usual**].

I knew that I had done the right thing in leaving this man
when he said it was over.
A domestic violent scene I would have continued to be until I
sustained a catastrophic injury because then the police would
have to assist me and arrest this man.

Victimized, however, not placed in a criminal lifestyle, I
begin to heal inside.
My mind started to define the man I now had in my life.

I must take in consideration that the abuse in the last relationship may cloud my thinking in this.
So I show him love and he shows me love and everything seems to be as it should.
Therefore, I do adore him and I will not bring this relationship to end because of the pain from another man.

EXTREMITIES STRETCHED – I REFUSED TO BE BY MYSELF.

NOBODY'S BITCH

I'll eject your dick from my cunt.
I'm tired of you causing me any kind of issues.
I'm not going to fight for this relationship.
Why don't you just leave me for this nobody bitch!?!

The confusion starts because he cheats and wants to slap me
around to keep me beneath his feet.
I will not be controlled while he is whoring and then beaten
because I know this.

I'll dismiss you from my life.
Discard the problems that cause me any kind of strife or pain
because you are no longer my man.
We shall no longer be involved.
You need to be with her.

Confrontational I was but now I don't give a damn.
He's belongs to a nobody's bitch and I don't have the itches
for that.

I know I can find me something better as well.
That's why I must get rid of him.
Oh, I know I could cheat.
However, I don't want him fucking me.
She may make him somebody.
Who cares?
As long as he gets up out of here!

AT THE MOMENT, HE IS A NOBODY'S BITCH [*AND I DON'T
HAVE THE ITCHES FOR THAT*].

Inception

A trigger eliminates repetition of yesterday and forever is
only a castaway perpetually lost.
With voice, I can decipher meaning continuously and not be
hopeless.
If love cannot breech hate, then unendingly my loneliness
shall be.
I am a woman in need of a mate.
So why am I alone eternally?

The stars in the sky express my desires for happiness.
They shout to me everlastingly excitement.
Continually, I try to always be positive but I have not found a
soul mate.
As it is, is this something that will be for evermore or is who
I'm with the threshold to love?

Thorough insight gives enlightenment into yesterday and
forever.
Therefore, I can depict true meaning out of what my mate
truly desires even when passion is not in his eyes.
If this is only for sex, I will know.
If this is true love, this will show.
Because there is nothing to hide, I would think.
Hence, why would this man feel the need to lie to me?

If I love, then should I be hurt?
This is what my heart wishes to know.

The moon in the sky conveys romance.
The requirements I have are the same as my mate's requests.
He has asked me to be his soul mate and he does not want us
to deliberate over whether or not we are meant for each other.
He says he knows we are meant to be together.

So I do not feel any stressors because there is no pressure with this man because he is truly the threshold to love.

SEPTEMBER 18, 2010

You will bring me roses in a pretty vase to my house for my
birthday because you love me insanely.
You will serenade me with soft music on my couch because
you are insanely in love with me.

All these things I perceive through the way you treat me.
This will be September 18, which is my birthday.
My age I will not reveal and the year of my birth is
unimportant but the love of my life is the portion.
He's not subjected to change and states he loves me
immensely.
Therefore, my birthday is an ultimate fulfillment.

You will hold me intimately and caress me throughout the
day.
When night comes, you will make love to me as if the world
is ours.
As the hours pass, I be looking in an hourglass and the
reflection I will see is that of love.
All these things I conceive though the way you treat me.

September 18 is my birthday and the love of my life is my
ultimate fulfillment.
This is for evermore and he truly adores me.
Hence, this year will be explosive.

He will be here forever and I will be his Queen.
Bringing me roses, serenading me, holding me intimately,
caressing me, and when night comes, making love to me as if
the world is ours.
All these things are perceived and conceived into our
existence by the way he treats me and the way we treat each
other.

ROSEMARY

The whore was cockeyed.
She had too many men in her life[**style**] and because of this
she lost her mind.
Her eyes became crossed and cocked and hands were
afflicted.
She was slued footed and big teethed.
And, when she danced, men loved how she rolled her ass.
They shouted: "*Boy oh Boy, I got to have me some of that
there!*"

She was 5 "9" and streamlined.
Her hair was long and she was always well groomed.
Her mother named her **Rosemary** because she said her
cheeks was pink as a rose and she was always happy, thus,
never forgetting about her.

She lived in a small town in Tennessee.
She would not leave because there she felt she had equity and
identity.
Other women did not care how many men she was with.
If she left, she may be threatened because of her sex habits.

Rosemary is now married and in a domestic violent
relationship.
Would you know she loves this man and even her mother
cannot get her to leave him!

<u>MOLLY SUE</u>

Rosemary has a sister name Molly Sue.
That bitch really knows how to cut loose.
Knocking knees with flat feet, Molly Sue make men beg for
her so hard you could hear them grit their teeth.

There was this one particular guy that came from Mississippi
that Molly really cared for and he seemed to adore her.
His name was Troy and he did many wonderful things for
this girl.
So on Molly's birthday he brought her a necklace and told
her this was a sign that they would be together forever.

Molly and Troy wore the pennants that hung and Molly wore
them fulfilled and everyone knew that she was in love.
However, Molly Sue loved to go out dancing and Troy was
extremely jealous and all the Jones girls, which there were
four, had big butts. As Rosemary did, Molly knew how to
roll hers.
Nevertheless, Molly did not tell Troy of this and unexpected
visit happen and Troy was told by Molly sister Carol Jean
that she was out in the City dancing.

Troy went to the Club Carol Jean named that Molly was in
attendance, which was Club Escape.
When he arrived, Molly was on the floor doing a strip tease
show and rolling her ass.
Troy became ballistic immediately walked onto the floor and
removed Molly and told her to go get in the car.
Molly went but told him not to hit her.
Troy came out the club told Molly she was going to
Mississippi to visit his mother for the first time.
Molly Sue looked at him and ask Troy was he out of his
damn mind.

She said he was going to take her home until he calm down. Troy rationalized and said he would in which he did and then they went to Mississippi about three hours later.

Troy mother, upon first glance, liked Molly Sue Jones. They really got along and Molly really felt at home. There seemed to be a Mississippi and Tennessee connection going on because Ms. Jones was getting to be known. Troy Banks mother Camilla Banks had no trouble relating to Molly because both were plus size woman. They talked about church, clothes, and being Christians.

At about 10:30 p.m. Ms. Banks dismissed herself for the night and Troy and Molly watched television when Troy asked Molly to marry him. Molly said yes and set the date as well. Molly Sue Jones would marry Troy Bennet Banks on January 31, 2011 in her home State of Tennessee.

Molly and Troy never got married. However, Molly became pregnant with a baby for Troy and Troy was killed by a drunk driver on New Year's Day of 2011. Molly had a baby boy on their wedding day, which was January 31, 2011. She named the baby Troy Bennet Banks Jones I. Nevertheless, to make a long story short Molly Sue Jones about six months later started dating Troy cousin Terry at his mother's Camilla's request.

Molly and Terry got married six months later and move out of the country to the Virgin Island's because Terry was enlisted in the Navy and was based there. The truth of this story will never be shared but it is accepted by both families – The Jones and The Banks.

Molly Sue and Terry Lyn Banks had three boys and three girls from their marriage and Terry adopted Molly first son Troy, which was by his cousin Troy three months after their marriage.

Troy Bennet Banks I was told of the loss of his father, Troy Bennet Banks, when he was seventeen and he knew then that he was blessed to have family as his step-father also. Inasmuch, he knew there was a secret kept by the Banks Family as well.
Nonetheless, it he felt it was really no business of his.

A POET'S LYRIC

Frankie is gone.
He took his own.
He loved Minnie too much.
He shot himself.

Minnie lives with scars.
In her head is one eye.
She realizes she should have left Frankie but she could not
give up.

Frankie's fulfillment fucked him.
He loved Minnie too much.
Satan took his soul.
Now in a coffin he lays cold.

Minnie cried out but Frankie did not hear beating her until
she couldn't breathe and then one day unexpectedly
something within Frankie clinked.
Paranormally, he began to see himself and he knew he had to
end his abusiveness.
As timing would have it, Minnie was getting stronger and
therefore, had the strength to leave even if Frankie told her he
would be lonely.

Satan has been in their lives for too long.
With only one eye in her head, Minnie looks at Frankie lying
in his coffin dead.

In a dream state or is this reality, Frankie and Minnie
paranormality?
One thing for sure this is a domestic violent relationship and
Frankie wants to end his abusiveness.

Frankie you are truly fucked.
You loved Minnie too much.
However, Minnie lives with scares and only one eye.
But Frankie, you took your own home and on Labor Day the
Parbarers put you four feet in the ground.

[*Farewell Frankie*]

To escape the reality of this relationship, I must begin to
think of me.
He seems to want me to feel as if he is the victim and I am
causing him tragedy.
This is so unreal to my identity to continue to let this man
assault me.
He slaps me around when he gets tilted.
He states that he knows I am cheating on him.
However, there is no evidence.
I am always where I should be when I am not with him.
Furthermore, he certainly knows of my whereabouts.
If he does not, Frankie finds me somehow.

The occurrence of domestic violence is an absurd melody in
Minnie's life.
She's controlled by her oppressor, even when he states he
loves her with his life.

To leave should not be hard at all but Frankie study prolongs
it.
He doesn't know why he has this need to beat Minnie.
He just believes that he's possessed by evil.

The precursor to this violent partnership is when Minnie
starts to take center stage.
Frankie feels that he should always be the leader in this
relationship so he verbally abuse Minnie as well.

He states that he loves her and cannot let her go but he wants
to leave now also.

Now Frankie and Minnie have finally separated.
Their lives together were a constant mistake.
Neither left without a scar...
Minnie lost one of her eyes.
Frankie was a mental basket case.
He left in a coffin on Labor Day.

[*Farewell Frankie*]

BLINDED – BIND

*Ms. Mary Mack – all dress in black – with silver coated
buttons – up and down her back.
She asked her mother for .15 cents to see the doctor for her*
sickness!

My eyes are on the prize because man despises me.
And even when I write these lines, he still feels he can
criticize me.
He states that he scrutinizes me because I have place myself
above other women lives.
Therefore, he must take mine.

Retribution through confusion is the best kind to have to get.
Man has made a mistake!

*Ms. Mary Mack – all dress in black – with silver coated
buttons – up and down her back.
She asked her mother for .15 cents to see the psychiatrist for
her* **mental illness**!

Affirmation is affirmed.
Action taken is I didn't bear arms.
And even when they, men, cause me harm, I have not hurt
anyone.

My constitution is to amend the wrongs.
Therefore, I sue to alleviate what I have lost.

*Ms. Mary Mack – all dress in black – with silver coated
buttons – up and down her back.
She asked her mother for .15 cents to see the clergy to pray
for* **this**!

You know it is right to straighten out your life and to show others what is gone.
Then the cost that is paid is staring them in the face and all has died and went home.

Ms. Mary Mack – all dress in black – with silver coated buttons – up and down her back.

BAKED A MAN

Patty cake - bake a man.
Put him in the pan and turn him over again.

He called me a bitch.
I said you didn't mean that.
I don't have to take your shit – you ugly ass idiot.
And you know what else, that's your mother as well.

Patty cake – bake a man.
Put him in the pan and roll him over again.

He began to beat me.
I stop him with my fist.
I hit him until he was senseless.
Never a domestic violent scene again because this man knew
he wouldn't win.

Patty cake – baked a man.

I beat his ass until I caved in!

AM I CORRUPTED?

He did not love me so I left him by himself.
He said he did not desire me so I begin to desire someone
else.
Now the only thing there is, is his memories.

****

Why does he follow me like this?
I told him it was over yesterday.
He had been following me constantly for three weeks telling
me he loved me and asking me to remember how it was
between us before he started to mess up.
I told him it was useless to reminisce.
He got mad and said he was not going to live without me.
Slamming my car door in irate, he told me if I did not take
him back I had made a damn mistake.

What are you to do when you are in love with someone else?
I know he is threatening to do something to him.
Do I skip town without his knowledge and tell my new man
to follow?
Or, do I take him back and cheat behind his back?

{*So*} we talk once again over the phone.
I told him I decided not to come back home.
He asked me was I choosing someone over him.
It was evident than he did not know about Stephen.
From there I said of course not and Carlos, I just decided to
come home.

When are you to know that you made the right choice?
I know I may get caught.

When I cheat, I tell Carlos that I going to be with a certain family member and from there he seems to trust me.
He may be watching me.
However, I do have private investigation skills.
I would know if he is.

Why is he this quite tonight?
Or, is it that I am becoming over self-conscious about what I am doing right now?
Carlos began to talk to me in a high pitch tone, asking me why it took me so long to come home.
He seemed to be trying to stay calm and then he said:
"*Brittany, I know you been seeing someone. Who is he, your new lover?*"
I responded by asking who was he referring to.
He stated the man with the SUV that you see at that Professional Building!
I was elated because that was not Stephen.
Therefore, I answered and said: "*Carlos, that man is my Dad and soon I will take you to meet him as well.*"
How come I am falling in love with Carlos again?
Stephen is still my other man.
I happen to see Carlos with his other woman and took a picture of them.
This is for when Carlos really find out about Stephen.
I will show it to him and ask him why he is cheating.
And, if we can make amends, we will then promise never to cheat on each other again.
This should cause a happy ending.

Today Carlos and I had our anniversary of being together for five years and both of us are still cheating.
He has change mates about three times and I still kept the same spare tire.

Neither never leaving their marks in the street, Carlos now does not follow me nor do I let him know that I follow him. He has asked me to marry him next year.

I have said yes, knowing that we are both cheating.

But I love Carlos and still desire Stephen, thus, therefore, I feel I can handle both.

I have thus far without any struggles and will continue until one of us get tired of each other - that is Carlos and I or Stephen and Brittany.

POST FALL SUSPENSION DRAMA

Tonight I'm so misty.
Sad because my man left me!
He said I was not being true and I had a new pair of shoes
and he damn sure was going to let me wear them.
Not knowing what he meant, I begged him to stay and he told
me that he was in love with someone else.
That is when he left.

In this box is my new pair of shoes.
I am going to put them on and wear them to see who can I
find to add to this life of mine and then maybe I'll be in love
anew.

Stanley and I were very close.
I felt he loved me so much because he was so possessive.
We did everything together.
We even work two blocks from each other in which we had
lunch every day at the same milieu.
We had our arguments and then we made up but now all of a
certain he is no longer in love.

With these new shoes, I must buy me a new outfit.
A dress will be my preference.
With some Sophia cologne and some new earth tone and then
I will take the town on.

My name is Verlena.
I tend to be a dream girl.
I like my world spotless – without a worry.
Stanley has left me but the beauty of it is the world is a
market place and I am out for purchase.

I brought the new dress – the Sophia cologne – the earth tone and I am wearing it all out in the Town and the City is loud. My girlfriend and I are full of cheer and watching in anticipation for every man that comes near.

Stanley is out as well and he is staring.
As he approaches, he looks menacing.

"Hello Verlena!"
"Yes, how are you Stanley?"
"I see you have on your new shoes. So you brought a new outfit as well?"
"Well, yes I did Stanley and now all is well."
"I want you to know that I am extremely jealous Verlena."
"And Stanley, I want you to know I don't give a damn and furthermore, do not start a violent scene."
"Wouldn't dream of it Verlena!"

A PAUSE

"Stanley, you just slapped me!"
"Let's go Verlena!"
"Okay Stanley and Stanley, your new love?"
"Verlena, you know you where her!"

The End

KINGDOM OF THE SPIRITUAL FREE

Wasting my time with this man seemed to be a thing of the
past but here I am where I said I would never be again.
Jeopardizing everything I have just to save his ass and then
he begins to cheat once more with the same crack head
whore.
So I told him this time it was really over and that is when he
shot me because he said he couldn't let me go.
Now six months later I am healing inside and this man is in
penitentiary doing time.
And, as this story goes, I have another man in my life.

****

My life is just a puzzle and that's a tree.
I will grow it into a kingdom and live within it spiritually
free.
Love will be the focus and hope will be with me.
I will always love man and live with him in unity.

I have suffered pain but I refused to give in.
I know God has ascribed me to be a heterosexual woman.
So although man may abuse me, I love him with my soul and
as I grow old, my tree grows tall.

My destiny is just a maze and that's a forest.
I will live within it as if it is my country and I roam freely.
Tranquility is the conception and affection will be ours.
I will be keen on his perception as I plant flowers.

I have seen hostility within my man and have been abused by
his hands but I refuse to give in.

God has ascribed me to be a heterosexual woman so although man may abuse me, I love him with my soul and as I grow old; my forest [will] flourish.

**

My life is my destiny and the puzzle is within the maze. Therefore, the tree becomes more than one and they grow within the forest tall in which the country is a **Kingdom** called the *Spiritual Free*.
Love is their focus and hope is with each.
All are heterosexual men and women who have been in domestic violent relationships.

This is the *KINGDOM OF THE SPIRITUAL FREE*.

SHAMBLES RANKS

He seemed to be so sensitive but I want to only show him
how I love.
Should I poke fun at him to see what he is made of?
Will he get angry and become irate and tell me I am childish
and ask me to stop acting that way?

Well I say to him: **"Baby know this, you wanted me so take
me as I am."**

Once I grow I become so mature and he asks: *"Why don't
you play with me anymore?"*
I stated: **"Well darling when I poke fun you said I was a
little one so therefore, I have no more humor of a child and
after a while I just may leave your life."**

He smiles and states now I know that is just a farce.
You wouldn't do that.
Embarrassing yourself would be such a disgrace.
I would beat you an itch from your death and get off for self-
defense.

I laughed and said yes Jeff you can get extremely volatile.
That is when he slapped me and said you are serious you are
planning to leave me.
I had created an illusion in my man's mind and he was about
to snap mine.

This was not real.
This was not happening.
I am snapping.

In my purse was a gun.
I shot him.

He's gone.

In self-defense, I stand as the police handcuff me.
Well I get off as Jeff said he would or will I be sentence to
life in the pen without parole?

[*Ridiculous travesty – what's your position in this parody?*]

HUMANOLOGY: THE SCIENCE OF HUMAN BEINGS

If he beats you once, he will beat you again.
When he says he's sorry, it's because he wants you to
continue to love him.
Once the abuse starts, it seems to never end.
This is called the science of human beings.

Margaret suffered from his licks for twenty years.
Then he threatened to kill her and she killed him.
Margaret now is doing life without parole and was sentence
at fifty-eight years old.

Sam took her shit until he could not take it anymore.
His problem was, however, he loved Samantha with his soul.
So on her birthday their story was foretold.
In the basement of their home, Sam, Samantha, and their
children lay cold.

If the world seems dark in your relationship, you may be
incompatible.
When you can't apologize to each other, the reality may be a
need for separation.
Once the verbal abuse starts, it becomes almost intolerable.
The science of human beings is the factor.

Calvin was a big man.
He had really large hands.
One day he became extremely irate with Cindy and hit her,
breaking her neck within a second.

Marvin and Alexandria was a dream couple.
He started doing drugs and influenced her.

Both of them became abusive to each other and on the night of their anniversary and argument broke out while Marvin was driving, which ended their lives.

The gray clouds of life are forever changing.
A simple fight can be so fatal.
Many times we see the world irrationally, never to rationalize it again.

****

In all the events and instances depicted above, the ones that survived states that they were truly in love and with their [soul mates].
The science of human beings states in peace they [lay].

Perilous

Keep trying to make up and he will forever be the cause of
your heartache!
Every time he beats you, you tell me you will not stay with
him another day.
Now once again you are packing ready to leave because he
said he made a mistake.
Lilly, you must know your life is at stake!

****

In this life journey, the pathway I take is that of sorrow and
memories of heartache.
If I find a token along the way, I know the Lord is my keeper
and my soul is safe.
As the Lilly of the Valley in my Mom's eyes, I strive to be as
strong as I can be internally so that man will not hinder me
and control my destiny.
However, I tend to love deeply and therefore, I do not want
to let go when I know that I should not hold on.

Yesterday, I left.
Last week, I left.
Two months ago, I went away.
Today I am returning as I did yesterday.

The same scenario is constant pain but I seem to be truly in
love with this man.
So the passage of life leads me back here and this time I will
not leave him.
I must make it work for us because of my children.
They are his and [T]hey are mine and we shall raise them
together as husband and wife.

This morning I walked out but I came back.
Last night I stole away without a sound.
Two days ago I took a trip.
Finally, I am returning on day three.

Jonathan loves perils.
He states it helps him keep things together.
He does not participate in criminal activity.
He just drinks and spends a lot of money on the children and
me.
And when he is high, he likes to fight.
Many times he has blackened my eyes.
But he has become calmer and wants to settle down.
Therefore, I know he will not make me leave to go home to
my mom.
The children love their daddy very much.
He gives them anything they ask for.

WHAT YOU THINK

To perform, I must know whether or not she loves me!
To stay calm, I will let him speak first.
However, both start speaking at once and plus, she never said
she loved him.

****

Why am I so sad?
I really love my husband.
But he does not want to talk to me anymore.
How do I tear down the walls?

Why does she feel a need for me to start the conversation?
I really want to know if she loves me by the way.
But she never approaches me to talk.
Why do I have to always break down these damn walls?

If unity is so hard to achieve, are they incompatible?

What does she wants from me?
I try to give her everything?
When we married three years ago, we told each other how
much we were in love and then the words were not said
anymore.
What made those words discontinue?
I really do not know!
But I want to hear them again and that's for sure.

What can I say to him to tear down these walls of silence?
The only thing we say to each other is not too much then
what is necessary and is put in a hello and good bye, which is
until we meet again.

The walls of silence must crumble and this marriage must become stronger!

Is their life union worth the sacrifice foreseen and the depressed state their in?

How come she does not ask me to help when she needs my help?
Why does she take on hard tasks by herself?
I'll just do this for her to see will attention come.
She must know all I want is her love.

Maybe I need to meet him half way.
He will never ask me this way.
So I will just leave something undone to thank him for his time.
I know he will complete any task that is hard and this one needs a man's touch!

This seems to be a good icebreaker and maybe a sex maker.
However, when they are in the same vicinity well they talk or do what needs to be done?

Oh, I see this was a hard task.
Evelyn did not finish assembling the china cabinet.
Therefore, I will do this and when she comes in she has to say sometime to me.

I see Dave is completing the task I left as an icebreaker.
This is the first time this has been done to save face over a very ugly argument.
I am not going to lose this chance of crumbling this wall of silence.
I will just say hello and thank him for finishing the assembling of the china cabinet.

"Thanks, Dave" Evelyn stated as she walked into the dining room.

"No problem love" Dave responded, quickly standing to give Evelyn a kiss.

"Dave, I am ready to talk, if you are?"

"Of course I am. We have been silent to long without passionate noise. Once that is completed, Evelyn, baby, then we can talk! What you think?"

"Dave, let's make some noise without saying any words, except I love you!"

The eyes of sparrow are the eyes that are shrunk.
When a man is mad, watch his eyes, my mother cries,
because he may cause you [some] harm!

****

I am in a domestic violent relationship.
I am beaten in some way by my man every day of the week.
If I run away, he finds me.
Now I have found that I must leave this geographical region.

I was raised in a poverty-stricken home.
My mother never married and raised us along.
But she taught us many moralistic things.
One was never stay with a man who beats.
She would say that could be physical and/or mental.
Get out when you know that he is just an abuser.
The signs will tell by what he says and the symbol is how
many times he has hit you and said he would never do it
again.
That Carrie said was number one and if he caused you some
bodily harm.

Now today is not just another.
I have gotten out of that relationship as I said and life is sort
of beautiful.
Loneliness is never present.
I have my belief in Jehovah and his effervescent as I raise my
son and daughter without a husband but marriage is not that
important.
A new relationship is possible.
I am not denying that I am available.

Only I am going to make sure I do not end up with another abuser.

As another chapter of my life begins, I have made the move that was necessary.
I live in the State of Florida.
Naples is a gorgeous place.
My children love beach bumming and making sand castles as I sun bath.
This is how I found my new mate.

Zephyr and I have been in a long-term relationship for the last two years.
He is a very gentle man and tends to guard how he addresses me.
This is because I have told him in detail about my last relationship and he states he would never abuse me, neither physically nor mentally.
I am so happy that he has asked me to marry him in which this is his way of proposing:
"Bytranica will marry Zephyr Cannon."
"Yes I will Zephyr" is how I responded, as romantic as ever and this girl loved it.

Zephyr and Bytranica was married on her 30th birthday, which was September 1, 2009.
Their first domestic violent scene happened six months after they were married.
Bytranica lost her life and was five months pregnant.
Their unborn baby died as well.
Zephyr was given life without parole.
Bytranica other two children, Candice and Angelo Devonte, lives with their maternal grandmother who will forever mourn over the loss of her only child - her daughter,

Bytranica Monique Hartford-Cannon, a lost soul though domestic violence but never forgotten.

<u>MEN</u>

Maxi Vaughn is a woman who likes to have fun.
She has many men in her entourage.
However, her mistake is getting caught!

****

Is it that I do not seem to be as strong as I should be?
Is it that they think I am to strong?
Is it that they want to control me or they want me to mourn?
Why do men try so hard to live my life?
Do they really feel my destiny should not be mine?

In silence I sit asking myself why men treat me as if I am a
little bitty child telling me how to live my life.
And then I think: *"Well I am Maxi Vaughn and I do not have*
to be submissive to anyone."

Once I get caught, I do not take the blame because I am not
in a relationship with any man.

However, [**the**] Priest has my attention the most.
He hits me if he thinks I'm being unfaithful.
It is always a domestic violent scene but I love the way he,
{**The**} Priest, fucks me.

Now Javier is hot.
He takes my cunt completely into his mouth.
And when he finds out that I am sleeping around, Javier
states he will beat me to the ground.

Oh! Maxi menstrual just went off and I am feeling kinky
now.
I like to be with Moses then.

He does magnificent things to me.
I let my wild-side show.
Anal sex is explosive.

[**The**] Priest is knocking at my door.
He is screaming: "**Maxi Vaughn you are a whore! I know that you are at home so open up before I kick the damn door down!**"
Moses, thank God, had just left, thus, I let [**the**] Priest in.

"**So you are at home along. I will catch you Maxi soon and then all Hell will break loose!**"
Maxi Vaughn responded: "*You know I love only you honey. You are my money.*"

Maxi left when Priest did and went to visit a friend.
Priest did not follow.
However, Maxi did run into Javier.
They talk and he told her he would be over to see her in a little while.
Maxi responded by telling him to call her beforehand to let her know he was coming.
Javier did not respond.

Many more relationships Maxi Vaughn do have but these written are ones that are real to her.
[**The**] Priest, Javier, and Moses are on the long-term and she works them in her life without any problems other than them being suspicious.
Maxi, therefore, has to pretend that they are just superstitious.
Little she knows - all will manifold.

THE SCULPTURE OF HER

Tears I cry.
So I wipe my eyes and try to stop the weeping.
However, I must express my grief because I just decided to leave my troubles behind me.

Many enemies I have because of the way I live and that's in the lap of luxury.
I am quite famous and my significant other is insanely jealous of me.
Lamentation is like howling inside, as I sing with music in the background and then I hear a chant from a man from long ago.
He asks me am I sad.
I tell him yes.
He takes my hand and prays a beautiful prayer.

"May the Lord Almighty remove the sadness from your heart and replace it with what you wish for."

Once finish, he kisses my cheek and departs.
I told him I will remember him as well, in my mind and also in my heart.

An old lady on the streets approaches me with an inquiry.
"My child, are you alone?"
"Yes I am in such of a home."
"Well, someone new will come into your life soon from long ago but you may let him slip away!"
In dismay, I started to run and shouted back, **"Oh, I have!"**

Up the road not too far Carleece saw her pass lover.

He was standing at the bus stop and she screamed loudly:
*"**Martin, I didn't mean for you to leave so quickly. Can we talk**?"*
"Yes, Carleece but I am about to catch the bus."
*"**I just have one question. Are you in a relationship now**?"*
"No, I happen to be single and looking for someone. Are you interested? Well you not walk out this time?"
*"**No, I will try to see clearer somehow**."*
"Well, here comes the bus.
Let's get on board."

Reaching Martin's place, Carleece begin to relax and he went to put his things away.
In the middle of the room stood a statue of a female who Carleece knew to be someone Martin knew and had sculptured.
She felt jealousy because it was not Carleece and felt the need to destroy her.
Martin entered the room and asked did she admire *The Sculpture of Her*.
Carleece asked: **Who is she**?

Martin stated his last lover who left him completely empty, however, now Carleece was there to remove the void and therefore, the burden was no more because the sculpture of her is always his woman in which Carleece was now that from this day forward.

Martin and Carleece seem to be truly in love.
She has found a new job and now is pregnant.
Martin has begun to sell more of his art and has opened his own museum.
Nevertheless, the story begins to spin.

***

The baby is born premature.

Martin is cheating and Carleece knows this for sure.

Happiness seems to be paper-thin but Carleece refuses to let the Devil win.

She loves Martin now so much.

She feels he was there when she needed someone the most.

If it had not been for that old lady who approached her with envision, she would have

let Martin disappear never to see him again, unless by sheer coincidence.

Little did Carleece know Martin was not the right man!

THE SCULPTURE OF HIM

As the night falls, Carleece is hurrying home to see has
Martin pick up their daughter from daycare. As
she was getting in her car she noticed a tall gay smiling and
then he spoke: "**Hello Carleece**." Carleece
looked around and was astounded to see the man that she
would forever call her soul mate and who had broken her
heart on that very day she reunited with Martin. She then
thought of the sculpture at home of *Her* and felt then that this
was *The Sculpture of Him*.

*

In the old woman's eyes was Damien, Carleece lover that
was no more.
A few hours ago they had broken they long-term vows and he
put her out.
She was despondent and lost and did not want to go home.
Too many problems to face and she really would rather her
own place.
Now four years later he has appeared back into her life and
seems to want to reconcile.
That is when she thought about Martin's cheating and
decided she would comply but she would do it secretly, since
he was telling lies.
Damien took her right hand in his and asked her to go to a
bar with him to talk.
She said she would and both entered their cars and drove to
the local bar.
Damien ask about her life and Carleece told him all was well
in which she let him knew that she was in a long-term
relationship and had given birth to a baby girl whose name
was Marlesha Cartina Dupree.

**

Damien knew Martin Dupree and he ask Carleese was she intending to marry him. Carleese responded and said no time soon for reason being I want to remain Carleese Monea Davenport a little while longer. Damien gave her a passionate kiss and they left together to fuck in a hotel room across the street from the bar. They were together for about three hours. Carleese would tell Martin she worked over-time and this would be often and Damien would supply the extra money.

***

Carleese was in a whirlwind.
She was now in loved with two men.
She did not want to let either go.
However, soon Martin will know that Carleese is being unfaithful as well.
This will happen through Carleese slip of the tongue in asking Martin for something that only Damien would have and that is his name.
Carleese called Martin Damien while asking for a board game.

****

Martin knew Damien was Carleese pass relationship that had ended four years previous, which was on the same day that Carleese and he reunited; however, he was quite because he did not want her to be aware that she had called Damien and he knew that he was cheating as well. Therefore, he would begin to keep tabs on Carleese to see whether she and Damien had begun their old flame and then he will end his and then he will begin to sculpture him.

*****

Martin followed silently and saw Carleese and Damien met at their usual hideout.
He was not too angry to find that she was really cheating because he knew this by her calling him Damien.
He went home and begun to sculpture him but he decide to camouflage his identity.
It would be a two-month project and then he would surprise Carleese.

******

"Baby, your soul mate," Martin shouted to Carleese when he presented her *The Sculpture of Him*.
Carleese looked in amazement and whisper very softly he knows that I am cheating.   ·
Martin then asked do you love him.
Carleese responded and asked, *"That is you Martin?"*
Martin response was a question in a statement of who else would it be, not Damien!
Then Martin stated to Carleese: **"I am just playing baby. I felt sort of funny the other day when you called me Damien while asking me to pass you something."**
Carleese inhale a soft sigh of relief because she knew Martin really was just suspicious and didn't know anything and then she stated: *"Martin if I called you Damien it was just a mistake. I happen to come across an old picture of his the other day and it brought*
back unwanted memories. Nothing big but depressing and I was thinking about a situation I left unfixed and hope it would not present itself because it was financial."
Martin responded and said he understood and if she felt the need to discuss it with him she knew she could.
TO BE CONTINUED

ENTER THE INSPIRATIONAL—MOTIVATIONAL CORNER

CULTURE, COCKTAILS, AND CUPCAKES

Let me get my nails done – [*Japan, Asia*]!
Taste some fine wine – [*Austria, Europe*].
Have a pajama party with my girlfriends and cupcakes are in.
This is where I will unwind and slow down to discover who I am.

Life span happens in such a way that if we do not recognize who we are spiritually we may never achieve any form of equity and identity.
Therefore, why not develop and implement a culture within your own world that identifies your female as a spectacular woman.

[*United States of North America*] I'm going to get me a new hair-do.
[*Brazil, South America*] I'll lose weight becoming refined!
I'm going to throw a party to bring in the New Year and there will be a lot of cocktails.
Thus, this will disentangle my mind from what I do not want to engage in.

Destiny is such a happening that the way of life is recognized by the ending.
If I do not do what is right for me, my artistic means does not make sense and money can be leaves on a tree.
So therefore, I write poetry as an inspirational – motivational identifier of me; hence, sharing my cupcakes throughout society.

I am letting everything go to show the world that I have found me. [*Africa*]
So calm down and let's chill out and enter this inspirational – motivational corner. [*Australia*]

From there, once my girlfriends leave from this pajama party; my culture will be fulfilled, cocktails will be put away, and my cupcakes will be recited out into space, as I fall asleep, so I will be refreshed to take on another day.

CHEERS TO CULTURE, COCKTAILS, AND CUPCAKES!

THE ANOINTING OF A PSALMIST

Throughout life we as people must come together and provide each other inspiration and motivation.
If we are thorough enough, we will find that we have many similar characteristics that can fulfill a common purpose.
Therefore, we must build a bridge of consensus.

****

Must I go to Church to find the Lord Almighty?
Does a Covenant damn me from not following it?
But I am a righteous person and I do follow a righteous path
so why am I damned by the deceitful man and his kind,
which is [**his**] woman?

I have been to Church and followed their Covenant but only
jealousy was expressed by the congregation.
The members whisper blasphemy in my ears and I turn and
told them not in here and they said to me: **"Poethics, you
know you live scattered the fence!"**
My response was that's why I don't come to Church and then
I got up and quietly left.

In the mist of my tears is the Holy Spirit in which Lord God
Jehovah is performing an anointing.
He takes me to the spiritual realm, which is an emotional
high, and tells me that I am a *Psalmist*!
In the most Holy voice I hear the Lord and he shouts in a
bellow: *"My wonderful
creature, my magnificent child – I anoint you to write
Psalms throughout your life as a healing tool when things
in life may make you cry or just not right!"*

Today I write poetry therapy to heal, to cure, to uplift, to bring tears of grief and bereavement, to inform, to reform, to motivate, for inspiration.

Inspirit is my soul and my mind is whole, thus holistically, I know that I have the courage to withstand any storm because The Almighty God informed me that I was his chosen one to anoint with the gift of Psalm.

So to all I will share a thought from The Lord Almighty, who all know in formal keeping is *Jehovah God Lord*, that your anointment is there if you are willing to walk a righteous path!

SAY HALLELUJAH AMEN AND BOW TO A BEND TO THE KING OF KINGS AND OF ALL MEN AND HIS KIND, WOMAN!

THE KEY TO THE GATE OF HEAVEN

In my possession is a key; one that I kept close to me.
Location is next to my heart by wearing
it on a gold necklace for all to admire – for all to see.
Many men have offered to buy it and women have asked me
where I came by it.
I decline the proffer and I tell my story [*of glory*].

*****

If I am to be delivered from the wrath of man, I must take a
virtuous path that leads me to my Creator.
Therefore, I must center my thoughts on God as if The
Almighty is really watching my every move in which this
ensures that I am a respectable being so that I can and will do
good.

This accomplishment is an upright and honorable way of life,
Thus, no wrongdoing exists and justification is why the sinful
becomes a life in a bottomless pit.

My story of glory is splendor that is so brilliant that I hold the
key to the pearly gates.
Jehovah gave me the key in my dreams and I brought it into
my reality by visual means.
The Key to the Gate of Heaven is a token from the super
natural realm and I cannot sell it to any woman or man.

If I am to be taken from this world in ascension, then I must
convey a belief in an entity greater than my existence.
My Creator, I truly know and I have been told, name is
Jehovah God Lord and laurels are in my life because I am in
the light of knowledge and the anointment of The Almighty
God.

Stardom and praise is fame made in which the triumph becomes grandeur.
The Key to the Gate of Heaven is a wonderful credit to have when it comes directly from the King of Kings, which man cannot shun because he only wonders what this means.

I have attainment now and will forever bow 'till my knees bend because The Almighty God has chosen me to achieve magnificent things.
Heaven is my destination and I have the key.
The pearly gates will open and I will receive my wings, as an immortal angel in Eternity.

[*The Key to the Gate of Heaven belongs to me!*]

THAT'S WHY

If God is not there to repair life as we make mistakes throughout destiny, our lives can be so fragile.
For this reason, we must, from time to time, find our entrance into an inspirational – motivational corner to repent and ask God for forgiveness.

****

My Great Grandmother was a Cherokee-Ute Indian who migration took her to her final destination – the Mississippi Delta.
In her telling of stories, she told me, Poethics, of a Great Indian Chief – Black Hawk of the Ute, Sauk, and Fox Indians.
She said he fought for what was right and took White men lives.
This was inspiration to this girl because White men had human suffered colored people of this nation for nothing but their own subsistence.
Now, this day and age presents the White man as superior but he is truly in transition.

Let's sing a song of triumphant.
Let's chant a chant of victory.
Raising our voice only to a whisper but once released, our voice becomes glorious.
Proud and jubilant we are.
Successful though what we stand for.

My Grandmother died when my mother was only a child.
Her name was Mae Emma.
She was an India-Negro and my Aunt Lola B. states everyone said she was very beautiful.

You know I would love to have seen her as my mother does but she is just delighted that Mae Emma gave birth to her.

Celebratory we are in my family for our bloodline.
Dominant to our heritage, this is Mestizo, Indian-Negros!
Exultant to our struggles and elated by what we conquer.
Mestizo sorrow is their strength and we are proud to be within existence.

My mother is mean sometimes.
She does not know why.
But she feels this is necessary to survive.
Her name I will not reveal, however, I write this poetry to share with her to help her heal.
If there is a cure to what caused this, I will unearth it.
In time she will become more of a loving person.

Gleeful we praise The Lord Almighty.
We are exulted because we believe that if we provide God with a pathway to our souls, we will only gain wisdom and never grow old.
Therefore, we say: "*Have mercy on them Lord because they know not what they do!*"
And, a righteous pathway we walk for a passage given to The Lord Almighty God to our core, even when **The** needs no assistance in the execute.

YOU MUST KNOW THAT THE SPIRIT OF THE LORD IS UPON YOU!

***

THE BOOK OF JUDGMENT

I am the bosom of man and the breastbone of woman.
To me you owe grace and honor.
Therefore, in your life transition did you repent before you
came here – to Heaven?

As I open the Book of Judgment, it states that you did not
say: *"Forgive me Lord for I have sin!"* –
When you knew the wrongful deeds you have done amongst
man and his kind, which is woman.

Therefore, I must damn you and your wings are rejected.
The pearly gates of Heaven brought you to me because in the
Book of Judgment you were represented with an almighty
deed but you did not repent before you proceeded.

Wherefore, The Book of Judgment closes and you must
leave!

GOD'S CREATED ORDER

There are people in this world that will defile it.
They believe they are God and therefore, can tarnish what
The has done.
Beware of them and pray for their souls because only The
Lord Almighty God knows.

****

In the Garden of Eden lay male.
And as the days past, The Lord Almighty God created female
and then, she lay beside male.

Everyone knows the story of Adam and Eve.
However, Poethics, will develop this further, to depict God's
Created Order.

What an honor for you to give one of your ribs.
Here I am today male because of you I live.
In the mist of this beautiful garden we stand as woman and
man.
My name is Eve and you are Adam.
I know because God has shared that.
We have much to do so we can get to know each other.
[We are] life companions in this world together.

We are God's Created Order.
We walk hand and hand as one while God tells us what needs
to be done.

So as Eve travels through the Garden she learns many things
that she brings back home to Adam so he may traverse the
Garden whenever he decides he wants to follow her.

As the days pass, Eve and Adam became tired seeming to want new adventure.

Adam set the course and Eve promise she would remember.

But some evil sidetracked Eve and she begin to think about a tree that God had said was forbidden.

Would Eve continue to listen?

On this particular day she did and went home to Adam.

A serpent lives in this Garden as well and she would navigate through Eden without mishap.

One day Eve crossed her path and this was next to the forbidden tree that bared fruit.

The Serpent said: "**Hello Eve! You seem to be hungry.**"

Eve stated: "**Maybe I am but what does that have to do with a serpent?**"

Serpent response was: "**Fulfillment is right there beside you. Why not eat to nourish yourself. That's God's well.**"

Eve Laughed and said: "**Well serpent you know that tree is forbidden!**"

Serpent responded fast: "**Eat eve and fulfill yourself!**"

Eve asked: "**Serpent is you for real?**"

And then Eve pulled a fruit from the tree and said: "**Serpent you eat!**"

Serpent laugh and sounded humanly and then she begin to eat.

Eve watched pleased and decided she would eat.

But the serpent really was not eating at all.

She had supernatural powers that camouflaged.

And once Eve completely ate the fruit, the Serpent puked and it was whole.

Eve did not even notice this and begin to trot home to tell Adam.

Adam and Eve are together this day when Eve asked Adam to travel with her to the forbidden tree that bares fruit.

Adam response was that he would and they went on this distance journey.

As they trek, she saw the serpent.

The serpent did not say a thing because she knew Adam and Eve destiny and therefore, the serpent was ecstatic.

Adam and Eve arrive at the forbidden fruit baring tree and Eve told him to eat.

He said no Eve.

"God said this tree was forbidden" and then Eve's response was: **"But Adam I have eaten!"**

So Adam refuses as much as he could but Eve's persistency took his strength and he ate.

One bite and a swallow and he heard God's bellow: **"Adam, you have disobeyed me with Eve. Why did you eat from the Forbidden Tree?"**

Adam reply was: **"Eve said she had eaten."**

God then question Eve: **"Eve why did you eat the fruit from the tree that was forbidden?"**

Eve counter was the serpent persuaded her.

God became irate and told Adam and Eve their fate and caste them out of the Garden of Eden forever.

THE END

MURAL

In the minds of men stand permanency that will destroy intelligence.
In the thoughts of women stood hope but man stance leaves no recourse.
Now women ask Poethics for her life as the choice!

****

Glorious is the pathway of a righteous woman.
Her journey is an ending that never finds a closure.
May she be strengthened by hope from Jehovah and in time
may life become aglow knowing tomorrow her man will
come home.

If sorrow was her bed pillow, she does not self-pity.
She walks on this journey along in hope that her man will
come home.
In her yard stands two Weeping Willows.
She states she planted them there about fifteen years ago and
when she feels sad, she stands between them and they weep
her soul.

In the mist of her tears she shouts.
She combines happiness and sadness as one.
And then she feels wind, as if the wind was saying –
"Gladys, stay strong!"
She felt an inner force squeezed her heart and she knew the
time had come for her to travel aboard.

Let us question her man.
Is one in her life?
If so, why is she not stabilized?
She is expeditious it seems.

Her excursions takes her too many places.
Therefore, she is not in stability.
She tends to leave whenever it pleases.

In this crossing, she travels to Mississippi.
Her mother home state and where she raised her children.
But surprisingly she has gone to her man and he has asked
her to marry him.

The story has no ending because happiness is always a
beginning.
So let's state that this is the Alpha of Gladys's transition and
the Omega is a mural pictured.

UNTIL DEATH DO THEY PART, GLADYS AND CHARLES RICHARDS.

RIPE

I must consume *The Word of God* as if it is edible, not just something merely to read, interpret, and then proceed within a righteous life because The Lord Almighty God is fit for human consumption and must be seen as the body fat more so than the skin (*The flesh of my flesh*).

THEREFORE, I am ripe for a blessing and cannot be curse anymore!

So I must bow my head and bend my knees and say Amen.

ANTAGONISM DESERTED

Strength before weakness
If you weaken my strength, I become stronger and my enemies are no longer.

****

The time has come in life for me to state I am who the Lord God Almighty intended me to be.
The time has come in my destiny for me to accept my curses as a blessing in enmity because the hostility that surrounds me daily has not hinder me.
But, although the forgoing is true, the time has not come for me to trust you!

It is within my ability to see inside the soul of man and his kind, which is woman.
Within that content, I depict the value of human.
But still I ask who am I to judge another human being in which my answer becomes: **"It all depends on what it means to me."**
So, my mind begins to travel on its journey.
I listen to what he or she says to me and then I sense a feeling of need, which is whether it is in advisory or just a response from me.

Lord, I know this may be strange but I do not do this to every woman or man.
It happens spontaneously and I find that this person soul has spoken to me.
It tells me whether I am surrounded by an end keeper or am I outside of the realm.
However the knowledge of the antagonist evolve, I somehow unearth love.

As a motivational-inspirational person, I have the tendency of a therapist.
Foremost, you may disregard that statement because I just may be the Psychic in the basement.
You see once upon a long ago I was told I could see into other souls that have passed and therefore, I would be able to depict the future.
In all, if I was to be truthful, I know the world and its people.
Antagonism some say I cause because I tend to know it all.
However, let's move on.

Now that I am discovered, I want to go undercover.
Maybe become a Cop and solve some criminals' troubles.
But, I am really too old and Sylvia Brown has develop that oval.
Therefore, I am more of a scientist and human beings are my subjects.
This may cause bad feelings but I am not dealing with haters.
Only the forlorn is around because if they are down I know how to lift their spirits, hence, assuring them that they can go on though motivating them with a Psychic Reading and telling them where they can find a safe harbor.

ANTAGONISM IS NOW NO MORE ONLY A DESOLATED EXISTENCE IN MY WORLD.

GEETA Dark Sun

The abandonment of the soul is the spirit lost.
God [has] foretold us that we will pay for our sins once his son hung
from the cross.
Let us not weep for the earth is not ours.
We are just here on borrowed time hour after hour!

GIANTVILLISM AND CITY OF THE BEAN PEOPLE

INTRO

A wonderful world it is contemplated Jake as he planted his seed to grow his beanstalk. He knew that this beanstalk would nourish many so he watched it grow. One day he awoke and the beanstalk was clearing the sky and he decided to climb it. Singing merrily to himself: *"Oh, what wonderful day to play with your evolution. I planted this stalk of beans and its growing beyond my conception. So I shall climb it to discover has it evolved another wonderful world beyond."* Jake was foremost a positive thinker. He began to climb.

DAY ONE OF JAKE'S ADVENTURE

Jake climbed the beanstalk that day. He discovered that there was life formed beyond but he was afraid to adventure further and promised himself that he would build the courage to go the step afar. He knew that he had to be well prepared for his adventure so on his descent down the stalk he began to develop his plan for his journey to continue. As always, Jake began to sing: *"Mm mm... The adventure I am about to partake could be quite dangerous; however, I must completely discover that place. I know that it may be my very last visit – the next – but I am going back to conquer it and that's that."* Jake begins to instill belief in self.

Jack's Next Adventure

As Jack planned he would make two weapons and use them if needed. He would take some food with him for his sustenance and a change of clothes for his comfort. He must travel lightly. He cannot be overloaded. This was an adventure to discover the beyond and then return home. He would set some landmarks as he journey within this other world to ensure that he could return to his beanstalk, therefore, assuring his returning home and thus, hopefully safely.

Day ten, after the discovery of this world beyond, Jake began to climb his beanstalk once again. Now know that this City that Jack was from had many beanstalks. Did Jack think he was only one with this discovery? Everyone had to plant their own individual beanstalk. Was Jack's the only one with a world beyond or did he share this with others? Secrets were known to be kept in City of the Bean People forever.

Well, now Jack had arrived into this other world beyond via his beanstalk. It was a flora place and no one was stirring about. He walked and walked and walked until he came to a cellulosic world. Amidst these cell walls of plants and algae was a cave like house. He heard loud snoring. He felt to see had he lost his weapons. He had not. Jake entered the house. At first he saw feet then legs. These legs were very long but finally he arrived at the knee caps about 6 minutes later. He knew then that this was a big, big person. He became afraid but tiptoed on. He discovered the Giant. He was not about to wake him. Jake decided it was time to end this adventure for now and return home.

It took Jack about 1 day to complete his journey home. Nevertheless, he knew he would be back to meet this big person. He had to so that he could discover this world beyond forever. Meaning, he desired the world beyond to be part of his constructed life and therefore, he knew he would fulfill his desire.

JOURNEY TO MEET BIG PERSON

Jake did not remove his landmarks on his journey home from his last adventure that took him into the world beyond. He would travel via these landmarks so that he knew how to get back to the Giant's home.

Two weeks later Jake went on his third adventure. His plan was to meet this Big Person and become friends with him, if this was possible. He knew his life could be endangered because he was a small man but he had to find out if this Giant could be his friend. So Jake went on his merriment way singing: **"This will be quite an adventure. The third trip to what I will call Giantvillism. It's quite a beautiful place to me, as I see life forming and then there's this Big Person. Giant he will be call, quite scary after all; however, very much worth the**

adventure and a connection to his world." Jake stopped singing and walked quietly, continuing on his journey, as he completed climbing his beanstalk.

As Jake continued on his journey to Giant's home, he constantly discovered new knowledge about Giantvillism. Everything was cellulosic. But he notices that some of these cellulosic things may be able to take human life form. However, it seemed that they needed triggering. An evolutionary world he had discovered with biological means and after he met Giant and they became friends, he would find this world's trigger point because it was necessary and should be develop and this is the premise he would live by and also influence Giant to do the same through his instruction, if needed. Hopefully, Giant may know how to do this himself but needed a motivator. Jake knew well that he was that and more. Jake perceived himself as quite powerful.

Halfway to Giant's home Jake felt aspiration and became aspirated and as usually, began to sing while breathing out. He continued his singing merrily and almost ran into Giant who was outside his home. Jake found himself no more than twenty feet away from Giant when he saw his legs in a standing position. Jake did a double-take and hid behind an object he did not have a name for but if he described it, it would be to him a big fossil plant maybe an artifact of this world. Giant began to move and it seems as if he was humming. However, Jake decided he was singing in his native language, which words sounded like those of a humming bird. Jake needed a plan of approach and while he was thinking, he fell asleep behind the big fossil plant.

JAKE'S PLAN OF APPROACH

Once Jack awoke, he began to plan his approach. As he was doing this, he noticed many things about the environment that surrounded him. He paid close attention because these things would help him plan his approach more accurately to Giant's being. This was home so therefore, it must affect him in some way somehow. The algae changed colors. The cells breathe and the air sometimes hyperventilated when it was required by the cellulosic life forming in Giantvillism. Thus, Giant could be startle and Jake could get his attention by talking to him this time until he knew it was appropriate to meet. That is when one did not fear the other. Jake expressed himself as the in-depth intellectual.

Giant appeared and Jake said in his native language: **"Hello Big Person. I have given you a name– Giant**." Giant looked startle. However, Giant said in his native language, which for whatever reason Jake understood: **"Are you here on a visit? Are you cellulosic as well or something else**?" Jake sense that someone or something else had visited here before so he asked: **"Do you have many visitors**?" Giant responded normally: **"Yes, of the cellulosic kind but I feel you are different because you chose to hide."** Jake said: **"We must get to know each other first and be comfortable with the knowledge that I am not like here before I come out of hiding. Giant, as I call you, I will know when that is appropriate or when it is time for us to meet in person. I will be back and we will get to know each other more. However, this time we must not because I since your apprehension and you sense mine. Courage will be both our stance and maybe the vibes will tell us that the next time. Do you agree**?" Giant says: **"Yes go!"** Jack found that Giant may be visually stronger than him but was not going to use that ability to seek him out this time. He asked himself why and left quietly.

These meetings took place for several weeks when Giant stated: **"Hello Jack and I do thank you for telling me your name. You may go but on your next visit we will meet in person. You know I am visually better than you and maybe once I seek you out the next time you are in my village I will tell you more! Bye for now and I'll await your next visit. I will know when you arrive."** Jake said: **"Thanks, and I will ponder over this for a moment before my return. Bye for now!"** Jack leave well pleased and [**the**] Giant sneeze, smiles, and leave walking in the opposite direction of Jack as if by sure coincidence. Nevertheless, Jake did not sense this.

City of the Bean People

The City of the Bean People is quite a beautiful place. It is such a pleasant environment that no one mocks it in any way. The Bean People create landmarks that are individualized and part of each individual's mind in which others cannot define. Jake has his own personal beanstalk as everyone does and therefore, this is how this is done.

As a life form, The Bean People remain little girls and boys even as adults in which age is just a number and mortal life is that of an immortal. The tallest male in the city is about 5 "7" and the shortest male is about 4 "9," however, this is the majority of the time. Jake was one of the rare ones. He stood at 5 "6 ½". The tallest female in the city was 5 "5" and the shortest female was 4 "7". Nefa, Jake's wife, stood at 4 "9" in which many of the females in City of the Bean People possessed the same height. Thus, one would know that Jake married because he loved Nefa as he did his own life. This is told because more than often in City of the Bean People marriage was chosen based on height and everyone want to been mated just right.

Physical fitness was not an issue. Because this City was individually bean stalked, everyone climbed and walked. Obesity was not seen. More or less, in City of the Bean People, there were fine specimens of human beings. Body tight and muscles in place, City of the Bean People was ahead of nations in exercise, healthcare, and life span with a low mortality rate. Morals and principality was practice though The Doctrine of Crop and Harvest. Each male and female had to adapt to this doctrine in their own way and integrate it into family once they became adults and mated in which marriage was mandated. The Bean People religion was denominational in which they called themselves Prosperus because they have lived their lives in abundance and prosperity since their creation and/or cellulosic existence, never being ill or poor always maintaining their subsistence.

Culture in Bean Town was part of the City bling, bling! They socialized and told about what was happening in their lives and party until sunrise. These extravaganzas [usually] happen on Thursday night and when all was tired; they slept until Saturday. When Sunday arrived, they rose and begin their weekly journey into meaningful lives. Some where Doctors of the Common Cold in which Bean People got quite often but never became severely ill because these doctors had magnificent skills. There were no other illness and/or physical maladies in this city; however, a child could be born with difficulty, if the mother concealed her pregnancy. Since marriage was mandated but did not curtail sex, this happens often enough to become a problem. The doctors then would provide the mother and child with a sanctuary and the father was mandated by elder law to marry her and that would bless the child. From there, whatever was the child's malady it would become a strength in which it could be either medical or mental but it would be extended to another place in City of the Bean People. Meaning, that this malady(s) would become a sacred beanstalk(s) in which the child would gain spiritual guidance and religious definition because an element(s) would be missing from his or her soul and this was needed for completeness of his or her human life form and no one knew of this but the Doctors and the Scribes. Once a Bean person did die, burial ceremony was carried out by Scribes in which they were dressed in the leaves of their Beanstalk and was buried in The Field of Lost Lives, which extended miles and miles; however, never ending until City of the Bean People expires.

The women of Bean Town usually were Cooks, Teachers, Nurses, and Weavers. The men were the Doctors, Scribes, and the Landscapers. However, these were not mandated occupations by gender and in rare occasions there would be indifference. There economics was based on a trading system but this was established through industry and agrarian means in which there currency became the leaf (prosperose) from the Beanstalk of Prosperity, which only could be obtained by trading with the Scribes and the more affluent Doctors.

Religious gatherings happen on Thursday as well in Bean's Cathedral. The Scribes would read from The Doctrine of Crop and Harvest and the Bean people who attended would be blessed for a greater existence in which this would prepare them to covenant in Bean Town on Thursday night. Their partying was very diverse. They did not drink liquor but had many things to drink and a lot of food to eat. Those that did not attend would be attending to last minute business in which the Scribes understood and blessed them with The Smoke of Missing Hope during Bean's Cathedral Religious Gathering. Once this was done all was well in City of the Bean People and Bean Town tinkled.

Jake's Return to Giantvillism

Now Jake was quite ready to return to Giantvillism, however, he wanted to be prepared for whatever. So on the day of his departure, which was three months from the last; he gathered has weapons and added a flask of merriment. This he would give to Giant as a gift. As always Jake begin to sing: "**I am going to give Giant a gift. A flask of merriment and he will enjoy this. Therefore, I'm on my way to Giantvillism and maybe Giant and I will travel beyond into his cellulosic world!**"

Jake began to climb his beanstalk, which took three hours to top. Once he finally made it to solid ground, Jake began to walk. He knew his way well now because of the eleven times he had visit Giant and this was the twelfth. Jake felt at ease and please with being here in which he knew that Giant awaited his return and that Giant knew he was coming [**this day**].

As Jake travel on to Giant's cave, he discovered that some of the cellulosic life form had evolved. He saw a little man building a house and stop to converse, however, the little man, did not seem to hear a word spoken so Jake tapped him on the shoulder and both the little man and the house he was constructing vanished. Jake walked on and came up on a woman with four children and she spoke to Jake. "**Hello, Jake! So, you return today.**" Jake was overwhelmed. She knew his name but he did not know hers. Jake responded: "**What is your name my lady? I do not know yours, however, you do know mine.**" "**My name is Melody. I am a gypsy. Therefore, I know things that Bean People do not.**" Jake became fascinated and asked: "**How do you know that I am a Bean person?**" Melody answered and said: "**Will gypsies have insight into others' lives or life lines and Jake with you it is your height. I must go now with my four and maybe I will see you again**

to tell you some more." Jake smiled and bid her farewell and not a goodbye.

"**About five miles**", Jake thought "**and I will be at Giant's house**." Humming and then he begin to sing because he knew this would make time leave much sooner. This is the melody he song. "**My life is that of an ordinary man. I stand 5"6" and have such small hands. But if I need to be as big as I can, I have another half of pint in me. My wife truly loves me and soon, yes I do believe, she be traveling with me to Gianvillism and we will make love in this cellulosic world as we did in Bean Town as teenagers. Oh, her name is Nefa!**"

Finally, arriving at Giant's cave house; however, Giant was not at home in which Jake knew he would wait because he was there to stay for at least five days, which his wife Nefa knew he would be gone for that long but no longer then fourteen days or two weeks. Jake fell asleep and was awakened by Giant's return home. Giant knew he was there and came into his home with a loud bellow: "**Hello Jake, glad of your return. I have a pleasant surprise for you. Some of the cellulosic life form has evolved in Giantvillism and with me is my cousin Maddy**." Jake jumped from his mat and states: "**I discovered this on my journey to see you, Giant. First, I met a little man building a house. I tried to talk to him but he did not hear me and when I touched him on his shoulder he and his house disappeared. Next, I met a gypsy named Melody who knew me immediately by name and by my people. However, I knew nothing about her. We talked and then she had to leave. So, Giant I am not that surprise but I would like to know why do you call Maddy your cousin?**" Giant responded: "**Well, Jake you see I am from cellulosic life form as well and Maddy evolved the same way I did. Being from a cellulosic life form one do not evolved as brothers or sisters; only cousins. Therefore, our family history in Giantvillism is based on the foundation of how we evolve. Maddy is the second of my evolutionary life form.**"

Giant, Maddy, and Jake begin to get to know each other. It seems that all the difficulty Jake was afraid of in getting to know Giant three months ago had been banished when the cellulosic life form evolved while Jake was away. Jake was learning about Giant's life though him telling Maddy about what it meant to be from the cell of the Big People. It seems that this cell came in many heights because Maddy was not a giant. He was about 6"1". Jake would say that women would think he was considerably handsome. Giant also said that The Cell of the Big People would evolve many more cousins within the next five years as adults in order for them to procreate and start families. Jake then spoken and told both that this is what happen in his world as well. Giant went on to say that many more life forms were in Giantvillism and their cells had the same capabilities and authorities. With all said, Jake thought: **"Hmmm, every world becomes different but then they are all quite the same**."

Jake's Two Week Stay

Jake Castle began to think about Giant and Maddy. Looking in his case he decided to write a melody for when he brought his family, which include Nefa (his wife) and his three children (Jake, Jr. who was named after Jake, Nefreda Maria who was named after Nefa whose name was Nefreda Marie, and Joseph), to Giantvillism on his next visit in which they would perform this melody for the Giant and Maddy. And, of course, Giant and Maddy would be included into this performance.

Jake's Melody

From the Big People cell in this cellulosic world stands Giant and
Maddy - two of the same.
What well they do with their knowledge?
Well, Giant states there will be more evolvement!
From the Big People cell in this cellulosic world, stands Giant and
Maddy; two of the same.
Why are they cousins?
They cellulosic life forms are from the Big People cell.
From the Big People cell in this cellulosic world, stands Giant and
Maddy; two of the same.

Do you think there will be more like them?

Will Giant speak?

I am in this melody and Jake calls me Giant.

My people have started evolving and therefore, more than sure, there will be more of me and Maddy.

Jake now knows of my hidden strength and that is through other's writings.

From the Big People cell in this cellulosic world, stands Giant and Maddy; two of the same.

Jake has visit Giant many times and now Maddy is here twice.

Family I bring for number thirteen and now we will tell what we have seen!

Jake finished his melody and went to where Giant and Maddy was standing. He did not say anything to Giant about his mental abilities. Jake felt he should wait to see would Giant ever share out or would he keeps this a secret. This would tell Jake what he needed to know and how to go when evolving continued. Jake pulled Giant's shirt. **"Hello Giant, I have awakened." "Oh, of course Jake; you are back and ready to journey with Maddy and I,"** asked Giant? **"And Jake, my real name is Herbert but you can call me Giant. I have become kind of fond of that nickname,"** stated Giant. Jake responded and said, **"You shall be Herbert the Giant and your name shall be shorten to Giant. However, do you have a surname or a last name?"** Herbert the Giant states: **"My people last name is Big People. Therefore my last name would be Herbert of the Big People, which you have substituted for Giant."** Jake ask, **"Which would you prefer, Herbert the Giant or Herbert of the Big People?"** Giant said softly, **"Jake please call me Giant as a nickname but my real name has to remain Herbert of the Big People."** Jake said, **"Well do!"**

The Big Person Stone

Maddy had many things to tell Giant and Jake but he had also one thing to hide and that was a secret he kept deep inside. Every morning Maddy woke with a glow and Giant would ask: "**Are you well Maddy?**" Maddy's response was: "**I am growing Giant and that's why I glow!**" "Glow Maddy, Glow; Go Maddy, Go; Grow Maddy, Grow!" stated Giant."

"**Reason being that I know Maddy's secret and he will kept this secret because it is just us two and never will he tell the truth. Nevertheless, the truth will be revealed when the stone of life plants a tree,**" song Giant. "**Maddy will wonder should he tell me.**"

Maddy continue to glow for about three years. He grew just as tall as he could be, which is 7 "3" feet. Cells were formed on this tree and Maddy wife was one from this blessing.

Giant did not seek Maddy for explanation but stated to Maddy he still possessed his secret and that is when Maddy spoke on the stone and Giant and he became blood. And all know this is when family was formed.

The Big People Stone created the monarchy that ruled Giantvillism. Giant would be the King and Maddy was part of the Royal Family. This was not known to Jake and his family and would be revealed when Jake returned in late December. Many surprises are in store for Jake of the Bean People. Giant and Maddy will be the presenters.

UPON REQUEST, GIANTVILLISM AND CITY OF THE BEAN PEOPLE WILL BECOME A COMPLETED TALE FOR EVERYONE TO ENJOY!

PARABLES

DON'T BE A FOOTSTOOL

A woman lived in the land of opportunity.
She had many influences in the things she did and the choices she made.
However, her one mistake was trusting when she should not and she ended up being lost.
You see she was blind by her faith and had to trust to make it.
Nonetheless, there is never a blind fool and because this woman knew that by putting others before self she was being abused, she begin to challenge self.
One day she went to a friend house who she knew was availing up to no good but she wanted to be certain that the foregoing was true.
Not knowing she was disadvantage in approaching this this way, she became even nicer.
What she lost was self yet the friendship was kept.
She never understood what she did wrong and her friend exploited her more.
It became so consuming no one could get to her and the woman lost touch with the world.
What is the moral of this parable – this tale?
Well, use yourself and let no one else in until you win.
Don't be mistaken as a weakling.

LINGO

As a platform of philosophy, I am standing on the back of Ghadhi, a foreign Indian.

Within this idiom, I think of a parable in which this is in the dialect of my great grandmother.

To keep all things sacred, a woman did not tell much about herself. She hides her life within.

No woman or man knew much about this woman and therefore, she was an Indian.

Her silence was her figure of speech and styled her life as she rocked softly.

Her chair always was place in a clear view and her expression was that of long-ago.

This Indian woman was known.

One day her great granddaughter asked her about her roots and she told her that she was of Indian blood.

Nothing else was discovered but this set a phrase to a heritage of language.

Indian-Negro vernacular formed and the Indian woman roots were reborn.

What is the moral?

A saying is always an antidote.

There's always hope!

|++++++++++++++++++++++++++++++∨++++++++++++++++++++++++++++∧++

STILL BORN

As people, we are not in a collection of minds but we are collecting minds.

In time, these minds will form structure and system.

Therefore, mankind must be humane and not destroy earth or themselves.

%/%|%/%

You see Joe knew he was wrong but he continued on.

This woman did not want him.

Her desires was for her spiritual life and because of this, Joe begin to lose his mind.

He harassed her to no extent and she did not let him have a damn thing.

Her soul and spirit was protected by the seeds she had planted.

The seed of life represented time.

The seed of inequity represented the right of wrongs.

The seed of hope represented salvation.

And the seed of peace represented war.

The woman felt a new birth must come and that is when Joe stopped harassing her.

However, Joe was part of her life and he did not leave that setting.

You see Joe belong to the same church and thus, they saw each other often.

Then the women seed of life formed.

Her seed of inequity righted her wrongs.

Hope seed gave her belief in God.

The seed of peace deployed.

Joe died in battle in Afghanistan and the woman revealed that she loved Joe even when she did not desire him as a companion.

And so, the spirit of Joe became the fulfillment of her soul because she felt sensual.

The ending moral… The woman did not have a vagina but still she was a woman. In the spirit, she hides her love. The death of Joe made her feel erotica because Joe, in life, had possessed her soul.

In sadness, she weeps and says: *"You know I will miss Joe."*

VIGOR

In former times, life was such a blessing.
Today, life is just smitten with a curse.
It all depends on you and your self-worth
******|******

When existence is verve and everyone is in a curve, you must become a
dynamic individual.
This was known by a gentleman name Vigor.
His affairs were of the heart and he knew his part, therefore, he became
a phenomenon.
Vigor took care of business and his preoccupations were his women,
which fascinated him senselessly.
He was so in love with one's ideas that he shared with the rest of his
bitches and that is when one of his whores became obsessed and she had
to be his only lover.
Vigor began to circumvent, when this bitch exploded.
She wanted to be with him more often but Vigor told her his desire for
her was no more.
Stalking became evident and that is when Vigor beat this whore.
He hit her with his fists and she became unconscious.
The factors became criminal but she did not let the police know.
Vigor began to desire her again and that is when she framed him.
Vigor vitality ended and this bitch enthusiasm made Vigor ask her to
marry him.
He did not know that he was framed and therefore, his other whores still
remained.
The bitch he married carried Vigor's name.
Vigor now is dead mentally, losing his vitality.
The ethical good that is seen is once a whore, why want God?

REPENT AND SIN NO MORE
∧∧∧∧∧|∧∧∧∧∧

A SINK HOLE

The future is an investment if you prepare for the worst.
Tomorrow is the day you have seen success.
There are messages in every passage I have read.
But Simon sees things differently.
He lives life as if he's a man in a bubble.
He finds the world troubled.
He does work but lives as a hermit.
He saves his money as anyone one would.
He never invests anything he should.
Simon states his life is secured and he does not trust and that's for sure.
The bubble Simon lives in is a lighthouse where ships dock.
Why he's trouble by the world is because he lost his family from the hands of criminals.
Simon hermit lifestyle is that of a writer and he is a renowned author in Seattle.
His family died because of the lack of financial stability and trusted when they were in need.
Simon lives vicariously, spending his money carelessly.
What does Simon not know?
His life will fold.
\\\\\\\\\\\\\\\\\\\\\\///////////\\\\\\\\\\\\\\\\\\\\\///////////////

A SAFE HAVEN DESTINY

Hilda version of life was that of struggle and/or strife.
She knew success but she always was in trouble.
She was a cocaine addict and she had no study man.
Hilda lived life as a scene.
Domestic violence had been a constant visitor when she thought she was in love.
The man she call her soul mate almost killed her.
Hilda is now alone and she does not want love.
In Hilda's life, she has had lesbian experiences but she does not want them indefinitely; therefore, she has only sex partnerships with men and women.
Hilda has a child.
She has been able to avoid the system through her child being often with her sister.
Hilda child is now fifteen and know her mother's history.
Raising one child has not been easy.
Hilda has her family love and they are loyal in helping raise Destiny.
However, Destiny does not love her mother unconditionally.
Many times she shuns her mother for her Aunt Veronica and that is when Hilda loses control.
Now Hilda has become clean and her and Destiny lives as family.
But because Hilda was not there when Destiny was young, Destiny disrespects her mother with her tongue cursing her for not being a good mom.
Hilda explains that she was there and provided for Destiny's care.
Destiny does not let go and that is when she negates her growth.
What is the moral?
Hilda knew she was in trouble and therefore, to leave Destiny in care of her sister, Hilda represented a good mother!
Destiny is in a mental struggle.
Nevertheless, Hilda does love her.

UNIQUENESS

Frequently my mind ponders on why diversification is not present in this country.

It seems to be an albatross to the government.

If the bureaucratic system stop and paid attention, then the economy would begin to flourish as it once did.

However, they want a country to stay in their history and make the White man more superior as well as the leader.

Wherefore:

A man became through White women.

His daddy was an East African.

He was said to not meet the criterion of being native born but he won the Presidency of a country.

He was seen as great before he even achieved greatness.

Norway awarded him a Noble Peace Prize for his distinctiveness.

Everyone in this country pretended he deserved the recognition when he was just elected into office.

He said he stood for togetherness.

His ways will bring economic awareness that well enrich us to our wealth.

Then everything became personal and now this country is economically depressed.

The government wants tyranny to succeed.

A democracy is never a character of one but if the unity is not one of peace, the morale of this country will become an economic disease.

His name is Barack Obama and he is the United States of America leader!

[*This was written on September 19, 2011.*] – Line 1 & 23

||||||||||||||||||||||||||||||||||||||\\\\\\\\\|||||||||||||||||||||||||||\\\\\\\\\||||||||||||||||||||||

PRINCIPALITY TO ASIA MALES

Mustering the strength of a giant, the man gave-in.
He could not move the concrete to different land.
He needed help to achieve this tedious task and that is when the construction collapsed!
You know that I want to be strong but I am venerable to the wrongness in the world.
You know I desire to be successful but I'm afraid to give up family support.
It's not that I can't adjust to the world I am in but it something telling me to withdraw within.
I sense a calling from somewhere far and if I listen it states: **"Turn your life over to God!"**
I do not respond but listen instead and that is when I recite a passage, which was written by me.
Lord, I am who you say I shall be.
And that is not a Priest.
But your teachings are my guide and after a while, I shall be realized.
In all, I know that if the Lord is for me, the world can cause me no harm.
*Therefore, when I listen, the moral must be: **"Adhere God!"***
@@@@@@@@@@@@@@@@|@@@@@@@@@@@@@@|@@@@@

[GOD'S HELL]
JEHOVAH GOD LORD'S HELL

FIRST TIER

To get a child as a child is never a healthy mind. When you were only three, you tend to ask why. From there you do not here an answer from those that carried the wrongful deed out. Hence, you start writing your first tier and maybe the answer will come about. Nevertheless, you ask God for guidance and take leadership of your [own] life. Living in the dude is not that problematic after all. Once you capture what is wrong, you will know that the mighty must fall. This becomes a mandate by *Jehovah God Lord*. YOU MUST KNOW THAT THE SPIRIT OF THE LORD IS UPON YOU!

This is just money in the bank, from your hands to my hands. I will fill my car up with petroleum and then this becomes my money to spend. Wrapping up this year [2010] with positivity and making money from cutting hair has become a real survival tactic!

****

"The Dude Look like a Lady" was written and song by The Rock –N- Roll Band **KISS**! To be duded means it is a way of life. Therefore, it is crucial that this **Union** vision becomes more clear and concise to the truth of what their participation has been and what society has went through. Stating that anyone can survive with a positive conception within their lives and that may just be the person in which they despise. So, let us just say that **Dude** does look like a *lady* but who is being played when he is not within your family.

Kiss [MY] ass and I do not need familiar[e]! Dude can do what he wants for you all here but I was not born for every life form that comes up until I die. Thus, the time has come for life to transpire and mine to transgress. Therefore, I must clean up the mess that was made in my home **State of Mississippi** from my remembrance of three years old forever to the disengagement of children from my lifespan and back into the trials and tribulations of man and his kind, woman, and all know that these are perilous times.

Hence, a philosophical role must be made – must be discovered – *The Last Forty*, which this is a generation gap in holistic belief in which this is a passage in the *HOLY SCRIPTURE* - **THE BOOK OF MATTHEW 24:34** states: *"VERILY I SAY UNTO YOU, THIS GENERATION [EVERY FORTY YEARS] SHALL NOT PASS, TILL ALL THESE THINGS BE FULFILLED!"* So, let it be known that I am the keeper of *Jehovah God Lord's Word* and I am in belief!

A notion is a model in society, which participates individuals when they hate what they know to be true and revealed, which this is the fulfillment that must come to pass, a transition that has happen through godly means and humankind cannot obstruct or prohibit through any bureaucratic means.

ONE CAN RELATE THIS TO CLIMATE CHANGE.

Many seem to believe that **The Sexton Family** is their family sexual oasis. Meaning being their well will never run dry as long as families utilize the *Sexton's Indian-Negro heritage*. However, a transition is being seen but men tendency is to fight to not face reality. Nevertheless, the world and its people are *duded* and that is the way it is to be.

To be within the world's struggle in which the world makes it appear as if you are at dire straits is just a pretense of what happen yesterday. Thus far, you have not been the blame of any of that that has happen but you are the center stage of nature disaster. **[So]** the Gulf leaked oil, there was Hurricane Katrina, still in the War against Terrorism; however, the budding of the trees continue to tell us the season. In hindsight, I must depict the future. Therefore, I must state that catastrophe is evident to the population of animals and people.

The theme once had it that this country would be forever enslaved by the white man as the majority and you know that I am speaking of the **United States of America**. Nonetheless, this country is a motif, today the white man with his white woman still claims the center stage and that would be in the sex industry, and the majority of the people let him. Nevertheless, once interracial relations take place the climax changes and the white man is only being fooled by his stance in a country. He must blend his identity in with the total culture of the people; hence, *America* becoming truly political-religious within its church and state creating an ambient surrounding in which each nation can be differentiated without the element of hate.

The sense of conviction is that certain sense that religion represents. When *the dude* is completed, the **United States** will be fulfilled with other countries [**free-world**] convicts and politics is only a penitentiary! Political-religion has manifest within a nation of distress. *Lyndon Baines Johnson* was the President that started this mess. He asked for immigrants!

DUDED!

Now let us journey into today and see what immigration has bestowed on the **USA**. In September 2001 the 11th day, tragedy was staring us in the face. A building in New York City, New York was a victim of a terrorist attack. The World Trade Center was a plane crash. This happen at the being of the millennium but a thousand years is how we should remember them. That people lost their lives from this catastrophe. In a century, human suffrage well surpassed what happen at the World Trade Center. It will become another sad memory. Within a thousand years, it will be well read history. As time moves on, we see ourselves in this country as the centerfold of other countries artistic expression. In this thought, this may be positive to our existence, immigration becoming a diversified caption and other countries emergence defining our talents. Therefore, we must speak of these countries via the Continents, which there is seven developing international relationship that may overthrow our super power. *America, the beautiful*, must see how this turns out! Maybe, we have lived in canine years. This country [**United States of America**] and its people will see as life preservers.

The next segment is that of tomorrow. As time develops the capsule, human expression may be the face of sorrow. Even when done in excitement, life foreseen as suffrage will become the enticement and the international picture is that of a terrorist trying to pretend that he or she is for the betterment of humankind when lives are constantly being deprived.

SODOM AND GOMORRAH!

Thus far, humanity has seen an element of *Jehovah God Lord*. Nevertheless, they ignore it. Developing more political hatred within their own nations in which implementation becomes that of fixation that states an abomination against creation because humanity wants the norms of society to reform to his desires and therefore, life is – will be despise. Let us note here that this is all seen through poetic eyes.

As a Psalmist, the eyes of a poet are universal to the world. It may be that he or she sees what many others do not. Therefore, philosophical prophecy tells all that a greater existence has evolved. In the bosom of **The Lord** is where this Psalmist resides. Knowledge being that he or she must be wise and show humankind what is scrutinized by **The Almighty God** in hope that the world will recognize *Mother Earth* as the destruction of our existence. Without her presence, our history cannot be mention! Earth as a planet is with godly intention. Humankind existence within this solar system, once falsification of the norms of society is successful, is the dirt and bones of their ancestors.

SCRIBES!

Apostles and Prophets stated to be amongst humankind today are only ***Scribes of Hindsight*** and therefore, do not foresee the future outright! They do not know when the second coming of Christ will manifest. Wherefore, to state such is false prophecy and will bring about famine and war. For some reason this is abhorred by God.

REPENT AND SIN NO MORE!

Evidence is that we as people must see our future through a greater global good because humankind has internationally mangled our goods. As nations have went further than export-import, illegal business practice has become the common resort in which we offer our help abroad when our country has lost. To salvage our souls, we must deplete human suffrage of any form and reform so that we do not bear arms on our own soil un-naming another Civil War.

In the name of religion, politics lay. In the USA, we remain Church and State. However, the human focus is Islam. Many do not agree because they are Christians and do not believe there is any need in changing faith. Does this mean what is at risk is the USA? No, it does not! What is at risk is the White race. Considering what White people have done in history, the face of the United States must be there pigmentation. Mulatto versus Mestizo versus Mulatto is 300 years in the making. History will see who is successful in changing the face of this great nation. Olive or Black is the token. [***Blood fulfills the portion***].

SECOND TIER

Sunday, February 27, 2011
Wherefore, THE BOOK OF JUDGMENT *closes and you must leave!*
****

In the world, there is a person who walks between good and evil.
His life is that of a Saint with many calling him Easy Jesus.
However, the Saint is not well formed when he has done so much wrong.
He believes Heaven is his home.

In a world, there is an individual who relaxes her mind from the life she lives.
She plays a piano and listens to herself as she strikes the keys.
But she is not that comfortable with herself.
She keeps her faith in repentance.

In the street of life, stands a young man.
He speaks out aloud and tells the world: **"I am the streets of perils!"**
He does not believe in God, only himself.
Does he, this young man, know his life is so careless?

God Hell is nothing like Satan.
It is the reality of man's crossing over.
Satan was only an Angel that was banished from Heaven in which this is where God lives and the righteous becomes immortals here.
God Hell is where the non-righteous lives.
With gates of stone garnet & pewter, the Angel of Immortal Death will guide you there.
All human beings that have sin and have not repented will go there for eternity.
The Book of Judgment may let you through but God knows everything.

Moreover, if you make it to Heaven and have none repented sin, God will reject you - denying you, your Angel wings.

Jesse was a bad boy but when he became an adult, he reformed. He was an advocate participator in Church and he really took care of home. He knew he was a Christian with a monotheistic faith. Yet he began seeking a richer way. Therefore, his sin became numbered and Jesse died before he was humbled.

Tamika was a very good girl. However, she felt that she lived in a rat's world. Therefore, to be successful, Tamika developed a strategic mind implementation became crime. Never being caught, Tamika's only fault was sin. Her crimes really did not hurt any woman or man.

Ashley and Ashton were fraternal twins. They grew together as identical images. Both played the same sport in school. Hence, an each had similar aptitudes. Once young adults, they began to do different things. Ashton became a religious man. However, Ashley began to live a fast life in which she was influence by the man in her life. Today Ashley has formed her life in repentance and has sought advice from Ashton. As a result, she has found God. Nonetheless, has Ashley repented and sin no more?

The doors of stone garnet & pewter open **GOD HELL**. The non-righteous must enter. If The Book of Judgment sends you to Heaven and you are a sinner due to non-repentance, God will not ignore your sin.

The will tell you: "*You cannot come in. For you have sin and repentance was not given because you did not ask for forgiveness. You must turn your soul over to the Angel of Immortal Death in which the Gate of Stone Garnet & Pewter will open letting you in.*

YOU BELONG TO *GOD'S HELL*!"

***

I am the bosom of man and the breastbone of woman.

To me you owe grace and honor.

Therefore, in your life transition did you repent before you came here – to Heaven?

As I open The Book of Judgment, it states that you did not say, **"Forgive me Lord for I have sin!"**

When you knew the wrongful deeds you have done amongst man and his kind, woman.

Therefore, I must damn you and your wings are rejected.

The pearly gates of Heaven brought you to me because in THE BOOK OF JUDGMENT you were represented with an almighty deed but you did not repent before you proceeded.

Wherefore, THE BOOK OF JUDGMENT closes and you must leave!

YOU MUST LEAVE!

IN PRAYER

Lord, my tears are not [**that**] of pain.

I have a greater lost within.

If I only could express myself without being criticize, I know that the tears will cease and my pain would be appeased.

Nonetheless, there is no love for me and I am alone in the world.

{*So*} Lord, I come to you to tell you of my troubles.

Jehovah sadness befalls me and I cannot see my way clearly.

I sense a need to talk; however, I have no one to converse with.

Therefore, Lord Jehovah, I come to *The* to remove what is not right and to walk in a brighter light of fulfillment-not forgetting the healing I receive with *The* as my leader.

My subsistence is based on how you bless me.

I am who you say I will be in my dynasty.

Forward I walk

Slowly I think

The fulfills the emptiness within me and thus, I will become freer to the faith that I am within and humankind that wants me to give in.

Desire is stated to be what is not given freely.

Hence, my needs are being provided by *The Lord*, and therefore, my desires will come.

I know this to be true and Lord, you can at will, use my soul to show the world that being alone is not known to their sense of being.

[My loneliness is a protective order from Lord Jehovah God.]

Lord, you have told me that I am your creature, your child in which humankind will condemn because I am of a greater existence [*then them*].

Lord, one day you will tell them who I am.

When that happens Jehovah, I will be embraced by the wind and civilization may fall because I am from [**I AM**] your child God.

Jehovah God Lord is the master of my soul and I [*IN MY DARKEST HOUR*] will remain whole.

In time, the world will know!

GRAPHIC

Once I was afraid but fear receded.
Once I was silent but now I must voice my feelings.
You see humanity has bestowed me with evil and therefore, I will
not forgive and forget humankind.

**

Moses freed the slaves of Israel.
Noah built the Ark and left in the flood that killed everyone in the
City.
He took two of the kind with him, who were gendered by animals,
and his family.
This is written in the Holy Scripture.
Thus, if God told it, you should not forgive and forget evil you are
bequeathed.

***

When you are hungry, you eat.
If you need guidance, why not consume a message from the
greatest leader.
God will prepare you for your destiny, even when humanity is
against your equity and identity.

****

You remember *The Word* telling about the two thieves on the
cross.
Each asked the Lord Jesus to not forget them because they were
lost.
Although they had criminal identities, the Lord Jesus promised he
would remember each.

The thoughts of mankind must be that of old.
Our history is our Bible.
In hindsight we will gain insight into the present, evolving the
future with our theories.
Let us see if we can change the world to a more conform image of
what the prophecies of the Bible represents.
Once done, our lives become the mural and the picturesque.
Blessed forever by what we do.
Abundance and prosperity brings forth the truth.

NOTHING TO GIVE – NOTHING TO GET

Choosing a man to walk for power must have been hard to find.
When you did, did you know in time it would not matter because
the world would come together to destroy what belief said was
necessary.
Nevertheless, great leaders died and thus, you chose a child.
Then the walk became magnified.
The talk was exploited.
Women and children were provided subsistence and men were
given jobs.
Nonetheless, we still remain in a Whiten world.

Are we sinking because we cannot transgress when the White man
has completed his transition?
Are we drowning because we cannot accept that this is a diverse
nation?
Are we blinded by fear when White people are only the numerical
majority?
Why do we not destroy what is not for this country?

The President, the Senate, the House of Representatives are all in
the mix.
However, they do not fix shit.
They continue to make a worsen state amongst explosive hate.
Then we are the people step forth and expose the retards and that is
when things begin to reform to deploying soldiers abroad.
The example is in the War against Afghanistan.
The sitting President blames the prior President for all but he does
nothing at all but continue the war to fight terrorism when we are the
people really do not know the real reason for deployment of our soldiers
abroad.

What is this country image to be, more international than
domestic?

What if we lose all the soldiers we deploy in active war?
Would this mean we have lost our superpower status to a society of
crime, which will not pay for soldiers and casualties killed; only be freed
by an ending?

NOTHING TO GIVE – NOTHING TO GET is evident when we cannot
protect our own nation from a terrorist attack so why are we deploying
soldiers in the War against Afghanistan!

THE WALLS

How many names are on the Vietnam Wall?
Why did we go into War?
Many lives were lost and now still we do not know the cause.
Will we ever be told why we lost these soldiers?
If we are, then the weeping will start.
Oh we cried and we cried but we have not truly mourned the loss
of these soldiers' lives in the Vietnam War.

We must expose God.
This is stated this way because the cause was untold.
On the Wall is the name of our soldiers.
We must claim their souls for glory.

The Koreans bared arms.
We went into that War.
Lost soldiers in a manifold and still we do not know the cause.
Oh we have cried and cried but our soldiers' lives will not reform
and we do have a Korean Wall disclosing the soldiers' souls that were
lost at War.

One day God will be revealed.
Uncovering of the untold will be known.
The Korean Wall will find its glory through the manifestation of
the souls of our soldiers lost at War and the doves will fly over the Wall
in display of what is shown: ***The lost souls of our soldiers going to
glory – going home.***

Today we are still in War in the Middle East.
We do not seek peace.
The sitting President stated there will be no more Cold War.
We fight to bring reform and conformity within the Middle East.
However, the above is not stated, thus we fight to stop terrorism,
which is a perilous thing.

War supposed to bring structure within a country once it rebuilds. The Middle East seems to be as is.

A Target

The hate that I feel is not.
The love that you feel has not manifested.
You don't have a snowball chance in hell to revamp yesterday so
why man are you trying to represent.
It is over with!

This City I live in wants to destroy me.

Love as an emotion you might as well forget.
The lack of feelings are what is evident.
However, if you want a performance of your feelings, you must
define what you feel when you express them.
Many will see that you are what you state, a mental poll of
mistakes.

The City I am within wants my destruction.

Now let's get back to what you despise.
In your eyes, you show emotions.
However, why do you not try to work them out?

This City wants to shoot me in the back.

I'm out of it because I refuse to be **A TARGET**.

A SPITE OF TOLERANCE

An interbred Indian with strains of Negro blood stands majestically
in the Black and White world.
She does not have many troubles.
She does have an amazing faith.
This is because in this Black and White world jealousy is stated.
Empowerment of a warrior has been given, as the people of this
world chants, she will believe us.

However, a spite of tolerance will manifest or this world will
deconstruct.
Reason being that Mestizo does not bother anyone.

An interbred Indian knows her strains of Negro blood.
She will truly mix this to become biracial.
Tracing her Negro strain of West Africa and her Indian to five
tribes, Mestizo will bring her image alive.
Via holistic means, her vibes will let no one in who desires to
disintegrate her godly grace.
As her face is sculptured by her cheekbones, she is at the highest
level of her heirloom.

Another means to a spite of tolerance.
The Black and White world aims to extort her for their [**OWN**]
means through her Indian heritage.
Nonetheless, this cannot be done without it been known; therefore,
she will continue to mix her blood.
This will ultimately protect her from the Black and White world.

Finally, Indian Individual Money is not desirous to her.
She is building her Mestizo legacy to enable her to destroy those
who are conspiring to live their lives unjustly through her interbred
blood.
[*THIS IS MESTIZO AND INDIAN-NEGRO*]!

ALONENESS

The words I am about to state are those which guide my faith.
In the world I do live, with God interpreted.
Reason suggests that I must compare my life to others.
However, I do not try when contrasting seems to take place.
Life is my amazing grace in which I accept what is wrong and do
not wish for more because my blessing are known by God and I shall
receive my just reward.

The master of my mind is the Creator of my life.
The focus I am in is given via a godly realm.
Therefore, my troubles are only a test by God.

If I express self with a vocabulary that is holistic, my words
become faithful.
The world will see the interpretation of God and life that is led by
guidance from above.
Suggestion is contrasting others that try to compare and amazing is
the grace that accepts my suffrage in which I live within the world but I
am of God.
Discovered by others that attempt to deny me what is attainable,
which effort is what worthiness becomes!
God and I are one.

The master of my faith is not in existence.
God is the chief officer in charge and dominant to the world.
If only I could share the expert knowledge I have, surmountable
blessings will be given.
Humanity would be the receiver.
Nonetheless, the world rejects what they deem to be truly anointed
because they do not want the world to be Godly.
Therefore, the world I am within, amongst humanity but God is the
leader of my life and humanity lacks guidance.

Maybe the sky will alight and my imagination will be the vision in other eyes in which I am the salvation of what may destroy mankind.
Until I die, this will be in everyone's life and the sacrifice may just be the end of civilization.
Live as if life is amazing and the maze is your success within creation.

Man believes he is greater than Earth.
He molds his life throughout existence as a never ending presence.
However, he does not like change when it concerns power.
Man will sustain a swift lost and the Earth will be what he is lying upon.

Death is inevitable.
Throughout humanity the mortality rate becomes the greater figure in the economy.
Why does man seem to think death is his enigma?
Death is only perplexity when you think you are eternity.

Power represents an eternal being.
Man strives to achieve it via money.
Yet, money cannot buy immortality and if it can, then it is man paradox and not a supernatural quality.

Inevitable is death.
The mortality rate figures are higher than the economy.
This is no mystery to man, although he lives life as if it will never end.

Questions should be asked of yourself.
No one is greater than Earth.
However, you can enrich your lives while you live by showing others what you have to give.
And, before you die maybe you will be known throughout eternity, if death is the way it should be.

AND AFTERLIFE AND A MEMORY

GREAT ARE THE PROCEEDS

"Grow tall child and after a while you will be a grown woman",
stated my great grandmother.
"I planted my seed by teaching you Indian ways."
*"Spirituality is within you now so don't let anyone deter your
path."*
"To God's home is where you are traveling."
"Bow your head in prayer when you need a private talk."
"God is always there to hear your blessings and troubles."
"In time you will know **Lord Jesus** *as stated in Acts 20:21 and he
well take you to his Father whom is Jehovah* **God** *Lord."*
"Thus far, my seeds are taken well."
"I see your spirit being created."
*"You will become a beautiful woman within and your appearance
will stun humanity."*
"Verlena, you are love by God, hence, show your love to others."
**[Lifting our heads, my great grandmother and I said "Hallelujah
Amen!"]**

IN SPITE OF THIS

SO REAL

I wonder does my mother have any regrets for what she has done
to her family.
Now she is sick and on dialysis and wants me to be sympathic.
I do wish her well, however, she is not.
Therefore, I try to provide some form of comfort so she well not
self-pity.
Nonetheless, she does not want any love from me.
One day I visited her at her home.
Gave her twenty dollars because she said she was broke.
Did she thank me for it?
The answer is no.
This is when I left feeling down.
It is not sadness I feel, however, it is the thought of my mother's
soul.
I hope she has repented and sin no more.
Nevertheless, I know she has not because she still wishes me
misfortune.
Hence, God is the portion.
As a little girl my mother molded my destiny.
She told men that they could use me.
Not for sex but for their homosexuality.
So in another medium [**now**] I live because my mother was not my
defense.
To her child bearing years, she had nine children in which six
lived.
I lost my oldest sister in 2009.
Now there are five of us who fulfills my mother's life.
Her grandchildren are sparkles in her eyes because she sacrificed
her children lives to live in her governmental lifestyle.
But Verlena and Derry departed from her self-proclaimed prophesy
and yet, her hate is only for her knee baby.
She express this when I come around and therefore, I do not often
because I live out of town.

Then again, even when I lived in the City she's in, I seldom visited to make a better friend.

As I said before, God is the portion and I pray for my mother's soul and maybe God will listen and not let her spirit roam.

THIS IS ALL ABOUT MY MOTHER'S TRANSITION HOME.

INSIGHT BEYOND STRUGGLE

This soul of mine is tired.
It has been through to many trials.
However, it is not in tribulation because God has refined me.
I am in the spitting image of my Creator and therefore, I am
blessed as Job.
In the event the Lord calls me Home, Heaven is my throne.
Why is the belly a pit for man to notate?
If I am to be a picture of a greater faith, I will nourish self with the
harvest of Mother Earth and this will be the blessing Jehovah gave!
My offering will be my body as Jehovah's temple and therefore, I
would not defile my body with street drugs and liquor serving God with
my spirit free of what is tempting.
My mind is suspended and I'm praying every minute because
Jehovah hears me and via my thoughts he teaches what is needed.
Thus far, my sin are repented and I am trying to not repeat them
showing Jehovah that I am righteous and my path is destined by my
trials.

AMEN

LIVING IN A PHILOSOPHICAL WORLD

Detail is what you see and don't see.
In life you just well be misled, if you did not pay attention to the
detail.
Therefore, if you want to be adequate, shut your mouth and start
listening.
Do not over talk yourself, you'll tell things you should not.
Please, get your foot out your mouth.

Just a little advice I am giving.
However, you don't have to be attentive.

If you tell everything you know will your life be known?
How do you keep your secrets when you are communicating what
you have seen and heard!
Sooner than later you will tell something on yourself.
That is when your life is no secret.

Everyone one needs a little advice somewhere in life.
And although your advice could have saved them from
unnecessary hardship, they do not have to follow what you say choosing
their own way.
Nonetheless, do not press; let them live.
The soul of humanity is always in struggle and strife, which forms
in the life you live.

The End

LOOKING OUT

My level of maturity is not known to humanity.
It seems to be desired but their lives were done different than mine.
And today knowledge brings that I am the one with all the means
and humanity does not have a [*damn*] thing.

Looking out I see the struggles of humanity.
Within a globe, humanity tells all that they are distressed because
they must complete what they have started.
Many years of ignorance now must become smarter.

Standing for what is not right is why mankind has no insight.
Trying to achieve through illiterate means is trying to read in a
foreign language you do not speak.
You stumble and just may fail but when all is said, nothing has
become attainable.

Looking out to find more enlightenment is not there when you are
wrong.
If you desire a positive outcome, even a crime must be clear-cut.
This assures that you get caught.

Categorical are men and women.
Decisive to one or more aspects, male and female is ascertain to
form within society.
If they do not, humanity will fall.
Then there will be no more **LOOKING OUT**.

MEN OF INDIA

Why do men think I am nobody to be concern with?
They seem to think I should be used at free will.
However, my mind begins to spin and men just do not win.
I tend to defend self until the end.

****

One day I shall be a wealthy woman living holistic in the world
with no troubles.
I will begin to grow my flowers sharing them with others.
When it is time for me take a philosophical stance, I will become
an Evangelist.
Insight I will have and the Men of India will be jealous.
Why do I say this?
Well, in the world that I live within, this is apparent to the truth.
I seem to be a Buddha of an ascertain faith.
With the characteristic of nirvana with psalmist fingers, Men of
India waits in silence.

Where is the sun when it is so dark during the day?
Where is the moon when you are walking at night without a
flashlight?
Why do men remain in darkness intentionally?
This is about the Men of India.

Knowledge is to men all over the world.
I am, however, in India.
This population is naturalized in the United States of America.
Men of India have a culture of religion and a monotheistic faith.
They seem to think this is not appropriate for Church and State.
This is why I state the Men of India is desirous of my intelligence
in which they want to hinder with a persistency that is ridiculous.

Men of India will recede and my political-religious presence will precede.
Men of India must believe that this is God deliverance and therefore, they cannot defeat the greater existence.

When the sun shines, why is one feeling dark?
When the moon gleams, why do the emotions not sparkle?
How come men seem to negate?
Men of India do not want me to be blessed.
If this is not so, why do they try me with sex?

In closing, I must state and reiterate that the Men of India does not control my faith and thus far, things are going the right way.

NEVER [SHALL I DIE]/ [NEVER] SHALL I DIE

If I was to live forever, I would be as bright as sunshine.
I would give a gift to all humankind in due time.
The world would belong to me because I am eternity and my life
has become a part of Mother Earth in which I am in the image of my
ancestors.
Descendent of servitude slavery and maternal to the natives of this
country, I will be as the day is to the night – inevitable.
This is my vision of life immortal.
If my life was forever, the sunshine would dimmer and once more
become bright.
I would gift humanity with the strength of love and the strife to
fight.
In war, we will be victorious though our belief in God.
Our reward would be what has become attainable.
If life was endless, it would seem as if immortality was budding.
We as people would not know whether we were mortals.
God would have gifted us within tomorrow and yesterday is
amongst the warriors.
To the world my life is incessant, a token of piece and
togetherness.
Blessings are constantly acquired though the capsule of time.
Repeatedly
Continually
Constantly
As always and at all times, I live life as if it is forever!

Sometimes the existence I am within starts to express itself.
In fact, this is happening quite often.
My body seems to be suspended in time and my mind is capture by
its setting.
Nevertheless, I continue to stay focus.
I do not believe in fairy tales but this seems to be the quotient.
If this is not, I am under an evil portion.

My eyes protrude.
My nose is keen.
I must find the man of my dreams.

My love is like an hour glass.
If I don't continue to fulfill my needs, my affair will never last.
My sadness never shows because I keep me a man to show that I
am truly happy.
And, therefore the effort becomes static – ecstatic.
I may not be with who I want but he fulfills my thoughts.
No Doubts

My tongue licks my lips.
I smile with pearly white teeth.
I must keep my secrets.

Emotional I have become within my man's arms.
Between statin sheets, he makes love to me.
Thus, I concentrate so I will not make a mistake and this
relationship will be on the long-term, even when I know he is not the
right one.

If I never find my dream lover, it will always seem as if I have.
My single-mindedness assures me of that.
Hence, my heart is not in it until I do but my main aim is to live the
life of a whore.

My scores will never be counted because one man can turn me out and when you see me, you will believe that I am sleeping around.
In my shadows, are all women!

THIS IS NO DOUBT!

Frustration operates the mind into a mold of self-destruction.
When you know anything you will be gone.
You better manage your anger to get alone.
Thwarting the need for success, you must prevent what causes
hindrance.
Defeat is easy to accept; vexing happiness.
You better eradicating what infuriates and move on to develop
hope and a greater way.

Philosophically thinking is all that it takes, establishing aspiration
to state: *"I have a goal to make."*

Flipping your mind into positive thinking creates an oval of
satisfaction.
When you know what's happening can cause exasperation.
However, it is better to know so you can eliminate.
Why would you want to remain aggravated?

Philosophical thoughts are worth thinking about when they enable
you to work things out.

Disturbance can be turbulence.
You will cry.
You feel moisture in your eyes.
Once you release the uproar, everything is fine.

Philosophy is more than a thought.
It is not just what you think.
It provides insight throughout humanity.

PITCH BLACK

Well, today is gloomy and I feel the environment as if it is me.
My life seems to be so misty.
I wonder if the sadness going to relinquish my emotions.
I know the element of clinical depression but this is just over the weather.
I need to settle a crisis that has come into my life; however, I cannot do that immediately.
The weather causes me to procrastinate when I want to end this today.

****

If I was as happy as I should be, I will go and do what is necessary.
I am involved in another person's life and I did not place myself in this crisis.
He wants me to give him me sexually to hide his homosexuality.

This is a story that is so rare but it is happening everywhere.

You see to introduce self I must tell my name.
It is Oblivion and the man spoken of above is not my man.
He is in my life via an organized plan that took effect when I was an infant.
You see, man wants to change the sexual norms of society and therefore, God will be victorious because they cannot defeat the greater existence.

This is a tale that is so real many will say it is fabricated.

You know to be a heterosexual woman you can discover the sexual abnormalities that is in the world.
To do this, does not maintain any activity that is so hard you must put your life into perilous times.

Just live and love and you will learn.

This is not a fairy tale.
What I am telling woman is real.

Well, it is left up to you to believe.
This is God's world and thus, it is not left up to me.
The greater existence becomes the entity.

APOSTLE STAREYES

What is the well of God?
How do you know you are following his word thoroughly?
The answer is you don't.
The Holy Scripture only teaches us right from wrong.

*

My story was told by many elders.
They stated to humanity my trials and blessings.
However, none told of the insight I foretold of God and Mother
Earth being as one.
Therefore, many were doom from ignorance.

In the presence of the moon, the world shook.
People begin to tremble from the quake.
As they heard a voice state, *I am God and this is the Earth I
formed.*
*If you do not adhere to my word, you will be spontaneously
combusted like the Dinosaurs.*

People begin to scatter with fear and all was quiet for many years.
However, there was one fool in their mist that unsecured the world
once again.
His name was Abraham and he knew how to start mayhem.
He decided people needed to have fun, unwind, and get to know
each other better.
He had a friend name Joshua and he was a minister.
Joshua already had his Churches in all of the cities with appointed
Bishops.
This was all going on in the world so Abraham decided to open up
Clubs.

In the world that I am from, there was population of one million.

When Abraham opened up his Clubs many stop going to Church.
God watched and listen in silence.
Church was not that important but the ways of humanity were.
Thus, God was in everyone's household to see which lives would manifold.
Every man and woman soul was theirs and their children were washed in the blood of lamb, even if they were disobedient.
However, what is the age of a child?
Zero to twelve and then their sin become theirs.

As mention before, the elders told my story of grandeur and glory.
I am a woman in this world and I saved the people from destruction.
My deeds are that of a Cathedral and Abraham is my husband.
His friend Joshua is my half-brother, which makes him Abraham's brother-in-law.
I brought Abraham unto God.
In my house, I designed and built a place of worship.
One night Abraham was so down about his Clubs.
I asked him to enter the Cathedral.
He did as I instructed and he told God his troubles.
And that is when God said this is a world of perils.

Further, *The Almighty God* stated via Abraham mind that he was not going to destroy the world because Mother Earth had entered perilous times.
People would have fun, unwind, and get to know each other better but the perils are that of danger, threat, and risk.
People will become criminal identities.
Abraham left feeling the spirit of God and he knew if he lived right he would be justly rewarded.

My brother Joshua was still preaching *The Word of God* and reviving those who had left the Church to be in the world of evil, he felt.

He constantly told himself that people had to live their lives and in time they would repent and sin no more.
He will be there to give them a Church home.

Joshua was very impress with my success with Abraham.
Abraham never left Church and Joshua knew he was a business man.
The elders watched over the world with their insight and I, Stareyes, watch and listen from the sky.
I have long passed but I am an Angel in Heaven and listen to the elders as they tell others of how the world manifested into perils.
And they, [**THE ELDERS**], do tell the tale quite well.

I AM APOSTLE STAREYES AND MY HOME IS WITHIN THE SKY.

THE HOLY SCRIPTURES OF HUMANITY

This is about my equity and identity.
Many think I am too holy.
However, I am only telling about what the Bible didn't.
This is about marriage and family.

****

In modern time, we have developed societies that manifested
communities.
This is how the family structure evolved through procreation and
mutation until we had massive populations.
Today, we have a Biblical presence in which human capacity
becomes communication and labor.
For this reason, our history is our Bible.
Documentation of how the family became strengthen through
documented marriage, conversely, is not the truth of it.
This is because domestic violence exists.
Yet, our bibliographies do make a difference in which common
law marriage is not a thing of the pass but you must know it is better for
the family if you have the necessary documents to prove your union was
historically fulfilled.
Humanity then stands a [w]holistic win.
Man and woman have written a Holy Scripture as time changes the
picture.
Mural though-out the world, we have realized that we are just like
the Dinosaurs and therefore, pre-creation is known.
Humanity must define the new world revealing our Bible.

You know, if I just could say what I felt, I would say it.
You know, if I felt what I said, it would be more effective.
Therefore, I write to express my inner being and my poetry begins
to scheme!

It becomes quite necessary when it is a need that must be fulfilled.
Reason being, you lack a certain element essential for your well-being.
Whichever is the case, you must face your demons as if they are another person closing this revolving door forevermore.
Once this is done, you have overcome.
This is ascertained to who you are.

It becomes quite remarkable if you win based on the obstacles you must defeat.
Logic is that sacrifice is not, only complications and stumbling blocks.
Therefore, excluding me now cannot be done.
You must pick up the earth and leave with it and I am suspended in time from the lack of gravity.
Do you think you will be able to succeed?

It becomes something of an accomplishment when the world belongs to you and I am not within it.
However, my life goes on and you own a planet.
Earth is the one you have acquired.
You are happy now.
I am suspended in time, never to stand on solid ground again because I am not loved by men.

******

The philosophy of [**my**] *life is* [**my**] *poetry.*

<u>Tinkerbell [Is] Dim</u>!

Maybe time will tell me if I am in love.
Thus far, it has only shown me pain and hurt.
You may ask why I am still trying to make it worth me.
I simply answer that even if it is not love, I do care enough to try to make it work.
He seems to think the devil is always amongst us.
He states that he does not know why he is so abusive.
I answer him by telling him he is just frustrated because of society at large and soon he will find a job.
However, the verbal abuse does not end.
He begins to take things within and withdraws from me and that is when the relationship ended.
In prayer I go because I must let go.
I must not become contended to what is not real for me; therefore, I have stated why this relationship must become history.
A never ending story that places me in the eyesight of Jehovah and tells me to steadfast to what I know.
A journey with God that does not end until eternity is seen.
A transition between me and a man, hence, I will love again.

Amen

TO BOYS

It's sad if you think about it.
So don't!
When someone does you, just leave it alone until you can rectify
the wrong.
You know God is guidance so read the Bible and you will discover
what you didn't know.
See the story was told about the Son of God and how mankind
denied that he was from the Great One.
The prophesy is that you must know your friends to overcome.
Life is just a vessel to explore the world and then make your
transition home.

Why not try to be yourself sometimes?
I know it's hard in this world of mine.
But you don't have to impress me with lies.
I love you for who you are and not for the man you think women
desire.

What if you found a million dollars today?
You turn it in but no one came to claim it as theirs.
You would become wealthy from a blessing by God.
So therefore, live your life right and you will be justly rewarded.

Life is an hour glass on a constant fill.
If it empties, you feel the stillness.
But don't dread because God is real.
When your time comes, *The* will make you a distinguished man.

To Girls

Turning the pages of the magazine, I decided that I needed to write
poetry.
Today is just another scene in the scheme of things.
Maybe a poem will release what seems to want to keep me a
captured suspension.

**

You know I am writing this to girls.
They seem to think they're on top of the world.
However, they are not because they do not know how many friends
they have.
You see the theme becomes know your friends and overcome.
But girls want to remain dumb.

()()

Holistic women are within the definition of the world.
Many seem to deny God.
They are being suppressed by man with their troubles when
Jehovah is there to take over their worries.
Girls one day will become women.
They must be taught though holistic means because once they
decide their path, women need a more refined meaning.

*

The story of an infant baby name Maria is told by many women.
In short the tale begins by saying that Maria mother was a single
woman.
Her path was that of a warrior in which Maria's mother would
raise her with her two brothers.

However, Maria mother died young leaving her and her siblings along.

Nevertheless, her mother did have an older sister that took them in as her own children.

On a cold day in December something strange begin to transpire.

Maria and her brothers were visited by a Scribe.

Their Aunt knew this Scribe well.

She told her niece and nephews to heed what he said.

The Scribe said that they would see the spirit of their mother in one year.

She would come to tell them what and why she left them.

Nonetheless, Maria, Jonite, and Kelem became scared and the Scribe knew this.

Each had passed the age of twelve but no one was eighteen yet.

The Scribe anointed their hands and then he left them with this parable:

Know when the time is to go to bed. {*GO TO SLEEP LITTLE BABIES.*}

Bow your head in prayer. {*PRAY FOR ALL GOOD THINGS.*}

And your mother spirit will leave you well taking care of you forever. {*AND IN TIME, YOU WILL BE IN GLORY.*}

**

Women now see their lives though men eyes.

They do not strive for a more feminine approach.

They do not feel the need to seek God.

They believe if they are quite and docile, peace will come after a while.

Never a voice heard in a righteous way only the need of man is being stated.

*

The moral of the parable is this:

Maria brothers were younger and she was the oldest.
The Scribe had told them how their destiny would unfold.
As their Aunt listen she knew that these children were blessed;
thus, *their mother spirit would be the first test in which their senses*
would be triggered but would it help them remember what had happen
when they were so young.
Remember this poem is for girls.

TWENTY-THREE NOT THIRTY-ONE

John Sexton and Derry Sexton are my brothers.
One states he is somebody and the other one is an alcoholic.
However, John does take care of self and that is all that is
important.
Derry is in Information Technology and repairs servers.
He has been married one time and has one child but Derry states he
is still dissatisfied with how his life has transgress in which he wants a
greater existence.

Family is important.
Now, I must speak on my brothers.

John is called Brer.
Derry is just Derry.
We all have the same mom but our dad belongs only to each one.
Brer's Daddy's name was Johnny Johnson.
Derry's was name Walter.
And, mine's is name Charles but I had a stepfather who I called
Shorty.

Family is of the utmost.
Therefore, I must speak and perceive via family.

John and Derry once were close.
Now they are a distance apart and one does not know the other.
Nonetheless, they do treat each other as brothers.
But the strangest thing is our Mom who grew us apart and
therefore, my brothers and I do not love each other.
Thus, because family is important, I now turn this over to the
Father and the Son.

Intelligence is a byproduct of knowledge.
Women tend to gain more from this.
Men tend to become more refined.
However, both will define what has been acquired once time has transpired.
Emotions have many elements that come from within.
Women tendency is to be expressive.
Men inclination is to keep theirs hidden.
Nevertheless, both will expose their souls through a threshold and then all their emotions are shown.
A need is always prevalent even if it is not yours.
Women mind theirs by the things they do.
Men are more manageable.
Nonetheless, both take charge and if they do not, they are more than likely to lose.
A child is born with embedded knowledge and apt to learn.
As an observer of society, you begin to wonder how come.
Then you think of how you observe anyone and know that God shows why a child must learn.
Wherefore, this is because a child will become an adult and all will see the byproduct called

INTELLIGENCE!

Jezebel was evil as hell.
She took many men minds and didn't give a damn.
However, she forgot about taking care of self and men begin to use Jezebel.

****

Oh, I know he's what I want.
I am tired of messing around.
I have sprung so many men because I am beautiful.
This man, however, holds a special place in my heart.
I must believe this relationship is safe and be faithful because I know I have fallen in love.

Jezebel once was evil.
Now she wants to please her man.
She's ready for a wedding ring and this is real she feels.

My promiscuity is still with me.
He knows of all the intimate relationships I have had.
He states he loves me because of them.
Therefore, I am ready to be with only him.

Jezebel evil has ended.
She states this with a feeling.
Nonetheless, is she ready to love only one person?
She says this is forever.

He is finally mine and I am going to be his wife.
In time, we will start our family and live happily.
Nevertheless, I am somewhat afraid that if I am not satisfied, I will find fulfillment outside.
In spite of this, I must move forward with my life.

Jezebel has an evil soul.
Her spirit will roam.

{ONCE A WHORE ALWAYS A WHORE!}

LIFE IS REAL

How is it possible that I am who I am and you are not the person
you say you are?
Is it probable that we are not chosen by God to carry out the deeds
that we have?
These are answers that we are searching for.
As we discover, we will get to know each other and that will make
this situation much better.

****

Taking life on a course of the unknown is fine as long as you know
what you are doing.
If you find that what you are doing is wrong, leave it alone and try
another route.

The possibility is always given.
Do you take it when you do not have the capabilities to complete
the things that are needed?
It is more probable to believe in what you do and if you fail, than
you can blame only yourself.

****

Giving in life is always done to what you know can help someone.
When you find that it does not, try to give only advice.

It is more than likely that you will trust yourself.
Therefore, your know-hows are those that are successful.
Thus, project what you do through your experiences and
proficiency will become the instrument.
Hence, LIFE IS REAL.

Living in the world should define humanity.
If it does not, then there must be a reason.
Could it be insanity that you are feeling?

Time shows and tells.
Be of the right mind, than humanity will win.

*****

Petrification of humankind is fear defined.
This is because the world is constantly in natural disasters that
we do not criticize; we prepare to keep our lives.
Do we believe that God is with us?
We don't have time.
We ask **The** for guidance via the mind.

The hardening of the soul is spirit frozen and therefore, the world
is cold until it becomes holy.

Ossification is our artifacts fossilized for remembrance.
Reason being tsunami, hurricane, earthquake, volcano, forest fires,
and tornadoes - these are all factors of natural disasters.
Do we prepare to keep our lives or pray for God's guidance?
We will lose via mind so why not prepare [*TO KEEP OUR LIVES*].

The soil is dug for our burial or we are burned and ashes are
spread.

Turning into stone is the cellulosic form.
What cause the effect could be the same as the Dinosaurs.
Our intentions are the things that destroy us.
Prayer may assist us in finding the right way.
Therefore, do not debate.

Ask God to guide your thinking and see if it is the way you figured.

In preservation is all singular sentences stated and thus, we are the memory of humanity through a transgression of thousands of years, when this poem was written that is.

SÉANCE

In a seat I am, trying to see within.
Should I ask what's wrong?
He does not seem to want me to inquire.
So I will not.
I'll leave and wait to see if he is still mine.

My spirit is with him and I know that he sense me but will this
make a difference.

We still communicate but his love is not there and mine's waits.
He states he needs space to find himself.
I know our sessions leave my scent and his senses see me.

My temperament is based on his and he seems to think we can still
be indifferent.

Deep in thought and sitting alone, he comes and awakens me.
Stating he feels a need to be free.
I quietly told him that is fine by me but I will not release his senses
until I am free.
He asked me what I meant by that.
My response was that my spirit still loved him.
He said well I know you will always be in my heart.
And that is when I said our union was in the form of a **SÉANCE**.

My soul is not fulfilled by inner self and therefore, you are the
keeper of my spirit.
Until my essence is not yours, my spirit will be part of your world.
It is nothing to fear and it is just our relationship gave me real
meaning.
This is because I fell in love and the ending of this bond has
disposition my heart and thus, I can let go but my spirit still will be
yours until I fall out of love.

I must depart now and say goodbye until my spirit says farewell.
Call me if you have a change of heart and I will let you know if
mine's want to still play the part.
However, from here I now release you from our **SÉANCE** and
hopefully I shall fall out of love.

Our nature seems to become individualize and he left with a smile.

CULMINATION

INTERMEZZO

I am the centerfold of your desires.
I see the passion in your eyes.
And when we make love, you set my heart on fire.

Man loves woman.
Woman loves man.
A romantic interlude that will never end!

I am what you want.
I see it in your possessive ways.
When we are not together, I think about you all day.
Then the night comes and we are in each other arms and that is
when the world is gone.

Woman loves man.
Man loves woman.
Romance is what they have discovered.

You are the one for me.
I am the one for you.
Our lovemaking has made me see the truth.
However, we do need to continue to grow closer and blend our
souls so that we can see a future partnership ending in marriage.
But if this relationship does not work and we have been together
for an extended period, our coming together was not as good as we
thought and therefore, we must move on.

Man loved woman.
Woman loved man.
Perhaps, romantically involved in which this does escape the inner
core of what love is made of.

TUHAN

True guidance is received when you believe in what you perceived
to be true.
This is because you have taken leadership over what you do.
In all, you must know whether your faith is fooling you.
Therefore, start analyzing self through TUHAN, which is the godly
presence.

In a realm you live.
In self you must believe.
A focus of something great to come is your establishment with
JEHOVAH GOD LORD.

The truth is honesty without any derivatives.
Your result is the end product of what is given.
All in all you have found your inner being.
As a whole, this is what you have achieved.

Scoping your life within your personal space brings self into a
range of greatness.
Divine Province you have found.
Your domain is godly bound.
When all is over and your life is seen before your eyes, you know
that your Kingdom is defined and you close your eyes.
TUHAN has truly been your guidance, justifying your trials and
you blessings.
This is when THE LORD does not question.
Find deliverance via TUHAN, true guidance from THE LORD!

THE BLOOD OF HUMANITY

The Book of Revelations showed the slaughtering of souls and
The Lord's Army was the carrier of the deed.
The blood of humanity would be the precede.

The blood of humanity rolled to the pearly gates.
The ending of time had come to pass as stated.

The spirits of humankind is in the blood.
Judgment day had come.
Jehovah and his son Jesus Christ Lord appeared and humanity was
gendered again.
Many did not see this prophesy in *THE WORD* and therefore, it was
not foretold that humanity would lose their souls.
St. John the Divine was found to be in a psychosis by a political-
religious person and she was the only one knew but she was not a leader
anyone would listen to.
Then the horrid came and humanity was silence by the armor of
THE ALMIGHTY GOD and life was taken from us.

The stillness shook and the people of the world rose and the Lord
passed down judgment and the Gates of Heaven squealed to prepare for
the souls that were lost to humanity but none entered because all was
with sin.
The Second Earth formed and the Lord knew that these people
would be immortals and live long lives.
However, eternity is in Heaven and Hell is where life truly
transpires.

INCOMPREHENSIBLE

The tower stood at least ten feet tall.
The City surrounded it with loud voices.
One man said that he knew the tower was about to fall.
Many were fooled because it stood with such power.
Then a noise was heard by all and not one could move because all
were startle.
The Tower split and bared the same and fragments killed one man.
Inside the second Tower was a King and his royal family.
This King had died many many years ago and his family was in the
manifold.
He became because of this one man soul.

It would seem to be a catastrophe.
This one man premonition was not to be.
All in the City was to be tragedy.
However, because a man foreseen the terror, a dead King is now
forever.

The people of the City began to disband.
The King of the Second Tower voiced his command.
This is when the people began to separate and the City became two
and each soul was changed anew.
Given new identities but within the same family, the people of the
Cities were governed by one King but this was not known.
The King of the Second Tower allowed the original City to
continue under their rule; however, he would be the entity within ruling
in truth, both Cities.

Many things would befall these Cities.
None would be able to feel a sense lost.
The King would take total control of their souls and their spirits.
In all, life would be empty.

The man that said he knew the tower was about to fall knew as
well what was going on.
The King observed him in silence and wonder why this man did
not feel empty.
The man spoke out and told many that death was their enigma.
The King heard and told one of his guards to bring the man to his
Tower.
The man went as asked and met the leader in the last hour.

But the paradox was the man did not know that the Second Tower
had form and the King wondered how come.
Once the King and the man was in conference, the earth begin to
spin.
The Cities went under and became another dominion.
The man became and the King was not.
The world they were in perplexed.
The man name was Joseph.

GOTHIC

The ocean waves became turbulent and the wind was high.
The night was misty from the waves.
As I walk in the moonlight, my mind became disturbed of what I
had seen in darkness and what it meant to the world.
You see I am a great leader and I must be of integrity.
The world will be threatened without my honesty.

/

A woman and man were in mystery.
All in the town knew nothing of this.
Many thought the world about him and her but if they were not
careful, the people of the town would be no more.
In darkness, I overheard their speaking of a certain disaster, which
would take place in Town Square.
Nonetheless, Town Square to this Village was the center of the
earth crust and therefore, this would be detrimental to the universe.
Meaning, the world could be destroyed in the aftermath.
The woman and man stated the mayhem would not even been
known.
Only the sound of the clock ticking would be heard.
The world's people would befall and animals would be more
powerful.
The great divided would become much less.
Animals would be our godly test.

DOMKIRKEISM

To get more out life, I must believe that my life is worthy.
To become more meaningful, I must get more out of life.
In all, I must believe in God and his deliverance given to me
though the life of his son, Jesus Christ.
But religion is not.
The Holy Scripture is in interpretation.
Spiritual relevance is the focal point.
Religion then can be found.

I have developed my inner core.
Implementation is within my soul.
All is done now in which I must show via a medium called my
personal world.
Spiritual religion I have formed and humankind denies what they
see.
And one woman would even ask for all to banish me.

The name of my religion has been established.
CATHEDRAL OF ONE TRUTH FAITH is identified.
Many can follow.
I will not know.
My religion (*DOMKIRKEISM*) was formed to create the inner core
as
well as a means in worshipping *JEHOVAH GOD LORD*.

THE BLACK CHURCH

I have a thing going on with prayer.
I will worship God anywhere.
And, if humankind denies me the time, I will visit *THE LORD* via my mind.
It can be in the workplace.
It can be within a shopping mall.
It can be on the streets.
In can be in the jail house!
When humankind sees me, I am in a glow because I am worshipping God.
Meditation is not evident.
THE LORD and I are truly together.
My prayer could be of deliverance.
I will pray for peace.
In prayer is my sense of release!
So people if you see me in deep thought.
If you see me not apparent to thought at all.
When you see me, I certainly will speak and therefore, depart a blessing.
This is because I am worshipping *THE ALMIGHTY GOD*.

THE GOVERNESS OF THE ALMIGHTY GOD

God has used the souls of his sinners since the beginning of
Creation.
Satan has been in Hell since God sent him there.
How do man figure that Hell is Satan domain for sinners?
God governs all souls even those of his sinners.
Humanity must see a greater deliverance from the evil of the
world.
In the Old Testament, humankind prepared and gave God offerings
for *The* to bless them and if they were with sin, watch their souls' clean.
Therefore, offered God something more as well as repentance from
the wrong you have done then you shall be justly rewarded.

*****

The Lord sent the spirit of a man who was demented into a swine.
The ate the Last Supper while drinking wine.
As I think of Biblical times, I know that my life can be refined.
Subsequently, sin is not part of my life line.

In the moments, seconds, or hours that I live and have lived, God
has enriched me as I am.
The see my soul in a transitive form so when I have problems, *The*
helps me overcome them.
However, no woman or man is without sin.
I repent even when damage has not been seen.
Sin can be such a simple thing.
But then someone else becomes at fault and God has told me to
take care of myself by stating if I do my best, *The* would do better.
Unto me *The* has granted my deliverance.
Accordingly and as a result, I offer my spirit and soul to *The
Almighty God*.

SPIRITUAL RELIGION

*Bringing forth the spirit of **The Almighty God** through The Holy Scripture to define **The** as the religion!*

God told man during Biblical times that a righteous stance fulfills all passages and therefore, spread his word amongst multitudes.
Currently, ministers of the Lord do not prepare the word of God into the interpretation of humanity but finds a way to swarm the word with ineffectiveness in which the attitudes become monetary gain and God does not mean a damn thing.
In Church you find this quite often and the ministers are only there for the offering that is suppose be to deliver *The Word of God* in a Holy Cathedral, however, it is not.
This money the minister finds is to make him somebody.
Comfort and convenience is what is going on in this Church home.

The Holy Scripture is *The Word of Jehovah God Lord* told by his prophets and apostles.

An Evangelist assembles to preach to the crowd.
And, as *The Word* leaves her mouth, she finds a sense of lost.
A hand touches her shoulder and that is when she spoke.
The words she stated was: "***God told me to come today to pray and bring deliverance to others***!"
Drive by shooters shot in the crowd taking many homeless people lives.
The word states: "***Surely you live, you must die***!"
How do you mourn when you know that these lives are better off with Christ?

Divine is *The Word of God.*
I speak to you all so that I know he's heard.
My ministry brings forth the sacred.
My sermons are writings of authority.

The Lord has shown me what my vocation should be and that is with *The* within humanity.

In the event you need a Church home, I now open the doors and bid you to join.

GOTTEN

The savor of something so terrific is waiting for you to enjoy.
The thing is, are you ready for it boy?
I know you say you can turn me out.
Show me what love is about.
However, it seems that you are scared of being hurt.
Don't give in if you are really afraid of making love.
The delight is waiting anyway.
Nonetheless, it will not wait forever and all depends on you and
whether or not you are together.

Relish what we have now and you will discover that we are right
for each other.

Taking pleasure is for the both us to do.
I'll love you the same way as you love me.
Therefore, savory is for me to enjoy as well.
I'll see if I can take your head in bed.

Appreciate what we have and we may just become one.

Delight in our intimacy.
You fulfill my everything.
And when I open up for you, you will cherish the love I am giving
you.
If this is not enough, we find more enrichment between us.

The value and treasure we have unearthed is what love is made of.

BYZANTINE

Should I allow this to go on?
Should I tell him it is over?
Should I find me a new man, even when I am still with him?
These are questions I constantly ask self because this man is
cheating on me.

/

The laughter was so loud and then there was noise outside.
I remember being here before, however, I did not know what for.
I was here today because my man had called and told me to meet
him here in an hour.
Then it occurred to me that this was where I caught him with his
mistress.
Why would he ask me to come here?
I step out of my SUV and that is when I saw him standing about
ten feet away from me.
He called my name and said I thought you were not going to come.
I asked: **"Why you thought something so dumb."**
He said in a solemn voice let's not disturb our memories and I
said I would not even consider reminding myself.
Thus, I asked: **"Why did you ask me to come here?"**
He said I have a surprise for you and that is when she appeared.
I stop and asked: **"You ask her to come as well?"**
I had not told him I felt that she was his mistress.
Then he introduced us as he did the last time and he told me that
this was who would design our wedding.
But the riddle of it all was her identity and that is when he told me
that she was once his mistress.
I ask: **"Since you and I have been involved?"**
He stated yes and no because no sex was being performed.
He said she was just another woman who held his heart.
Well, this would not be your mother?

No, this is my labyrinthine and she is still for me to discover and you are the woman of my dreams who I truly love.

I don't know why I love her so but she is someone I must keep close.

However, I love you in a different way and this is why I am asking you to marry me today.

I need to disclose this to you because I want you and her to become best friends to help me see why I need her in my life as well.

I responded and asked: "What if our relationship becomes convoluted?"

He said: "We will move to Africa for I can have the both of you. If you will take me as I am, I know we will be happy together."

I am afraid I cannot share [I said] and I left the "*Brother*."

SPORTS

The atmosphere is chilling and I am feeling the excitement from
the cause.
It seem be a course of action that is done to destroy me.
However, I do not fear what is untrue.
I know that if it is done the enemy will lose.

/

I have been involved in some evil doings.
It seems to be that the world is unglued because I have broken
through.
Many plots were composed in my life but I have defeated the ones
that were direct.
Nonetheless, the frame has become wood and the picture inside is
the nemesis only of self.
Why is this to be?
Well, my mother is her history.

It is a fairy tale going on.
And I am not overdose from the portion.
Stay in India America and this frame shall crumble.

I am clear of the evil in my life.
This is apparent to who tries to undo what I have done.
The schemes have become a revelation in my poems.
Nevertheless, the wood frame states she is together but her picture
says she falling apart.
A nemesis is her inner core.

Fairies are visited now.
She overdosed by their pagan sounds.
Women of India are in her house.

In a voice, the wood frame picture states she has found evidence to bring the pass back as today.
In her mind, she fears no one because she is above the law.
She does not know that what she is sporting is a fool's game in which she is the only one to pay.

Men of India are the nemesis.
She feels that I will forget.
Of course she knows her destiny is not mine, however, her belief is that the pass will revamp.
Why does she think that?
Ask Faye Thomas!

THE WHITE CHURCH

The holy man sits with his hands in a fold and then he rose.
He speaks in solemn voice to the congregation and said the truth
would be told.
He feels he is an Apostle of Christ and not God because our
salvation comes from the Son and therefore, he will provide us
purgatory.
Presbyterian Minister is he and he sees glory.

This is a White Church that I have visited.
My thoughts become that of the White man history.
Living in the United States of America has he repented?
Human suffrage is still his image.

A Catholic Priest was saddened by things that could not be
changed.
He was up in age and had seen many wrongful deeds.
One begins to think why is he saddened by this when he has
witness human suffrage?
Did he try to do anything to change the lives of the colored?
Since I individualize, a thought emerged and I knew these things
were of the world.
Therefore, the question must be asked of all [white] Catholics and
their ministers.

Is the White Church of God or just an imitation of religion, which
fools only White people?

White ministers materialize to diverse what they do to other lives.
Do they pray as THE BLACK CHURCH does?
I have seen and heard only [those] reciting THE HOLY SCRIPTURE
and then depart with a prayer.
The White Church needs to pray from the mind because God
does live and that is why we are here White people.

Then they will feel and see their forgiveness and justly be rewarded by God through [**their**] repentance.

STICK WITH GOD

I have the spirit in my soul and I must tell the world how my inner core was formed.
You see humanity wanted to cause me some harm and I went into pray to JEHOVAH GOD LORD.
I did not even have to ask.
THE ALMIGHTY GOD already knew my troubles and therefore, THE departed the knowledge and my spirit materialized bringing forth wisdom not known to mankind.

THE ALMIGHTY GOD fashioned my mind into parables to share throughout the universe.
THE spirit became the center of the earth.
I felt it and I felt others did as well.
Therefore, I continue to sally a godly blessing and humanity seem to listen well.
The lesson I taught, however, was not well keep.
Humanity continues to live perilous.

My spirit became what mankind could not understand in which evil became the portion.
Nevertheless, I continue to share my parables.
Wisdom I gave and humanity did not succumb to the lesson they learn.
They sally forth with negativity.
Now, mankind became the male gender and female was his identity.
Nonetheless, my spirit is my equity.

LORD GOD JEHOVAH is almighty and THE shall be the insight within that is diverged and when life is ending and my time has already digressed, meandering will be over and you must form your own inner core as I have.
This will enable you to share parables as well.

It is Just Not Right!

I use to be Dred Scott.
Now I wear Dred Locks!
I once was inferior.
Now I will kill and this can be physical.
In all, I am still in a struggle because this world I am in stagnates the colored.
It is just not right for wrongness to be in my life when you said in 1964 that all of us had the same rights.
It is just not right for the world to be against the colored living as they should.
Via the mind and spirit, this life is understood.

I use be enslaved but was freed via a secret passage way and later emancipated.
Now I am a great leader for my people.
I once was nothing.
Now I am educated and proud to be who I am which is from a nation of nomads and the oppressed man.
In all, I am who I should be because destiny is shaped by mankind and humanity sometimes is just not right.

Something is wrong when people think their lives should be fulfilled by yours.
They mind has gone and your life must go on.
However, it seems to be that man thinks of me as his deliverance and salvation from him identifying with his sexual drive in which he sees through homosexual eyes.
In time the male shall be denied because it is just not right to yearn to live though someone else sex life because he cannot live up to his sexual desires.
It is something of the insanity to say my life should not be mine and you can live it better than I.

It is just not right to be so full of fire and man wants to suppress your life for his to ignite.

It is something of the insanity for male to think he can take my sexual identity.

LORD GOD JEHOVAH, IT IS JUST NOT RIGHT!

SUR-REALITY-SURE REALITY

My heart stopped and I mumble to myself is this for real.
I had seen many things in my life but this was blatant and done
before my naked eyes.
I did not even do a double-take.
I saw him when he took what was forsaken.

/

The sundial was on high noon.
The moon was its eclipse.
I walk with silent feet and did not speak.
In the moment of silence, I heard a voice and this voice was
mystical.
It seems that the Princess was the girl name and her mom thought
she was a Queen but she was only a whore over a brothel.
This one daughter she birth was her pride and the joy [in her eyes]
and therefore, her brothel was never scrutinized.
She married her father and he never knew that she was rich
because of her looseness.
Every Sunday morning she went to Mass and that is where she
developed her talents.

/

The moon kept medium light and therefore, he burned a lantern at
night.
It was as dark as gray and the owls sounded the night away.
Yet it appeared to be sad when the man was happy to be by
himself.
He had his inner being to keep him company and that is where he
would meet his lover.
None would ever discover his secret because it was within and
who can journey there!

/

In modern time, the sky was pitched with blackness.
In spots seem to be eyes watching you.
The paranoia was a deep feeling inside until you saw something
unreal happen before your eyes.
It became paranormal and you were afraid to tell that you had
witness another dominion within yourself.

****/****

Who will ever win in this psychic realm we are in?
Nobody can when it is just mankind playing with their own minds.

THOROUGH

A man saw three boats and needed a ride home.
He did not ask any of the boat owners to give him a ride home.
He did not trust anyone.
One would ask was this man lost and because he did not trust,
would he find his way home without swimming ashore?

/

To trust is to depart with something so valuable that it is more than
an offering to God.
Should you guard this with your heart?
If you do, how will you become powerful within the world?
You must trust someone and that's for sure.

To ask God to guide your path is correct to your trustworthiness.
However, who will you trust, only yourself?
Does this mean that man should earn your confidence in him?
Trust is worth the deeds you fulfill!

================

A strange occurrence happen to Joann and what was wrong was
she did not feel she had anyone she could call her friend.
Her confidence was not even strong toward self.
She felt she was worthless.
Her family was not for her.
She had many hidden talents she did not share.
So God sent her somebody that seemed to care.
However, she did not trust.
Her life had not shown her happiness.
Therefore, no one could become close.
Joann life closed and all hopes were lost.
In spite of this, the person God sent did not stop trying.

She broke through and saved Joann life.
Joann has now seen success and her life is worthy.

Thinking moralistic, what did Joann learn?
Well, a friend is always sent by God.
Then again, this is based on the destiny you are in.
Friends are made just the same.
Nonetheless, even in that, your deeds are how friendship is kept.

To trust is a must or you may just withdraw from the world.
Therefore, trust in God.

There is a ruby hidden in the grass and I am going to give it to my favorite pal.
It will tell him how I feel and we will become better friends.
We will be constantly together until the end.
He will marry me and that's the thing and therefore, the ruby will become my wedding ring.

RED

I lost a ruby in the grass and I am going to find it to give it to my favorite gal.
She a love me with a passion and never leave me after this.
I make her my wife and we will be together until life ends.

I found a ruby in the grass and I am going to keep it for myself.
If I do find me a lover, he will not be told of it.
I wear it on my hand as if I have bought me a ring.
And, if someone ask me about it, I'll tell them that my man ask me to marry him.

I lost a ruby in the grass and I am looking to retrieve it.
It is so rare that if I see it, no one will be able to deceive me.
I'll tell them it is mine and ask them may I have it.
If they do not give it back, I will not attack but start legal proceedings.

This ruby I found has been there for many years.
It belongs to no one and therefore, it is make believe to say you hide it.
I have made it mine because of my discovery.
Your legal proceedings mean nothing.

DERAILED

Who in the **fuck** do men think they are?
Do they believe they are above God?
Why do they try to hamper **Woman**?
Is it because she is the righteous one?
When will they realized that the only life that is jeopardized is the
one who is scrutinized?
In all, why do they continue to try to change the ways of mankind?

A man was riding a bike when a woman asked him why he did not
tell her where he was going.
He stopped his bike and got off and said I did not know you
needed me to do something for you.
Yesterday you paid me five dollars and I do work based on what
you offer.
I responded to him by saying I was planning on paying you ten
dollars but that was smallest amount I had on me.
Then I gave him seven more dollars to add to the five and
therefore, he was paid twelve and that was more than well.
He said he would finish cutting my hedges and I can trust him.
I said will that's good because I did not **fuck** you.
But then he began to talk as if he forgot himself.
That's when I bid him farewell and he finally left.

Why do men think that **Woman** should be scared?
Fear is only for death!
Once you are dead and men have been conceptive, what will they
have left?
Not even a memory but a mental state, which says you are the one
that killed all you had and thus, you will be the aftermath.
You the ass!

LABYRINTHINE

What is a woman to do when she have so much manly attention?
Does she ignore it and play ignorant?

Or

Does she respond and pick her enigma?
Whatever she chooses, it is her choice and man must know that!

What is man to do when he did this?
Does he remain ignorant to what he has done?

Or

Does he take his woman?
Whatever he chooses, it really is not his choice.
Woman must want him as well!

Well, if woman and man do become involved, for how long?
Is it a relationship that was overdue long ago because man has
wanted her since he saw her?
This intricate mystery and puzzle both...
They accept each other for what it is worth and convoluted their
relationship to a more elaborate standard, however, they never married.
What you think happen?

THE CLEANERS

What I need is after it is done.
When you do it, however, you get nothing from it.
So why do you try to use me forever is a question that states to hell
with it.

You heard me shout out that you were my cousin.
But blood is nothing to you.
So why do you think I am your oracle is a question that states your
Uncle is my father.

Traveling to Memphis to take care legalities, I reserved a hotel
room and you stayed there with me.
Our journey took us to our home state and that is when you stayed
away.
So why do you think I want to stay where you are is a question
that states so I can get another witness to lie for me.

In all, we will leave and return home and that is when another
arena opens.
And thus, our companionship will be over.

SENTIMENT

There is a lose end I have to fix and this has to be done immediately.

If I had of known that all was trying me, my patience would have become paper thin.

However, tendency is to trust anyway when you know how your destiny lays.

Therefore, as you move forward, you know this is strategy until you stop them in their tracks.

Why have they tried to use intelligence when they only tell lies?

It would seem that they know that I am slowly becoming acquainted.

They take this as some form of mental hindrance that they have gave me.

Only one knows where her world lays and therefore, she will take her time.

This is to ascertain what has happen is corrected, her wellbeing is projected, and minds are not neglected.

Once mind is lost and everything else becomes right, Poethics will not allow human suffrage but one has to deal with why they are mentally suffering.

No one should be put in struggle when they have done what they should to avoid strife.

Why does mankind desire to live within a swine and say he is normal yet, you see a deranged mind?

SWAY MY WAY

It's a treat to feel the air hitting me.
The lights went out and it was so hot.
I wanted to strip myself naked to sooth my thoughts of how the
heat was about to make me go off!
My clothes were sticking to me as if I had soaked in molasses.
When I shed them, I'll put on something more comfortable and I'll
feel the air hitting my ass.
I knew my skin was sweet and the fire I felt was from the lack of
electricity.
The heat was upon me.

It is such a treat to feel the air upon me.
The heat was hot but now I have cool-off and my thoughts have
soothed..
I putting on clothes with toeless shoes and I am about to leave
these surroundings.
Thinking of a place where I can relax, I ended up on a deserted
island.
Music playing in the air and people are dancing with someone else
they might not even know.
But shelter of bodies communicates that you are not along and that
is when the wind blows.

Last night I was at home without lights and the heat was
smothering.
Today as the night falls I think of how lovely it would have been if
the wind had blown when the heat was so suffocating.
However, it did not, and tonight the wind is so overwhelming
because it brings thoughts of my lights out and my windows are open
but no wind is circulating and I went off!

Economically Diseased!

Just an obscene world with obsolete people and when I am out
mingling, I sense the emptiness surrounding me.
Such simplified means with complexity is my focus.
If I had a suggestion box, I'll place it out there somewhere
and tell this world of people what is missing.
It would seem to be that it has to do with the economy.
The deficit is ceiling and hunger is represented.
Being in forty-eight states with a district, attorneys are not the
greater intelligence.
Economists suggest that we must go further in debt to pay our
working class people.
Politicians know that we in a sink hole and may just be the fall of
civilization while other nations continue to grow their economies as the
cash flow.
Bureaucratic is no means to fix things but just a gap in the way we
think.
Somewhere there is an outsource and a civilian voice to give his or
her point of view.
The suggestion box that I set out will be given to a top official and
maybe then they will find an answer to why we are so behind in paying
our debts and this will assist the federal government in paying our debts
as well.
The face of our people should be that of ascertain wealth so why
do we have the highest deficit?
With this said, the poverty index will increase and to become free
of this economical disease we must cap our spending for as many years
as it take to win our freedom of owning money to others and not taking
care of our children in a country form to prosper.
Nonetheless, will this ever happen when White men do not want
another race superior though their prosperity?
He feels he's the economic genus of this great country and things
should remain the same.
You know {*White man*} a lot races are ahead of the game!

A REPROBATED MIND-PART II-THIRD TIER

This country that I live in has suppressed culture that will never be departed to man.

For some reason, no one gives a damn about themselves.

They express a need to end humanity with the ignorance of caveman tactics.

Their minds are thinking backwards.

Aren't I'm about nothing?

You wonder why I care.

In the name of humanity, I am just a humanitarian that knows what will happen in which this is a massacre.

Annihilation is by far what I feel.

I am a philosophical prophet and know that mankind is blood bathing themselves.

Mass destruction is the extermination of the American way.

Therefore, why is United States carnage to separation into a political-religious nation?

Meaning, you are killing us as you are.

You are ridding yourself of what the Founding Fathers stood for.

It must be a tiresome thing to be able to stop our growth but can't.

Is it that your butchering is only of yourself and those that follow your success?

Decimate your hate is what is being represented.

The world will be devastated if you win.

Mankind reduced to wimping babies.

It happened in Iraq and now they are refugees in Egypt.

I was told by the media that the devastation mentally disease them.

So now it seems the same is in place in American History.

Before it happens, we will execute the leader who has thrown away the Constitution.

The Supreme Court needs to be multidisciplinary.

This will provide this country with what we need to ensure our structure does not fall and failure was never a component to fear.

Our foundation was formed for prosperity.

We must establish greater truths through composition of our thoughts and manifest them in the way we say we are.

This may be deadly to some but leadership of right from wrong
will be the victory in the time of war.
This is apparent to fighting in the Middle East.
Benevolent we are because they are uncaring.
Afghanistan has gain many victories.
The sitting President states the Marines will withdraw.
Did our compassion help after all?
Well, let me move on.
[*No*] I have more in my tone.
The quality of life should be worth much more.
Our founding fathers asked for us to let others fight their own
wars.
Because we did not keep truth through the composites of our great
leaders thoughts, many of Americans platoons have lost their lives at
war.
In character, we are now and we must develop a tendency for
ourselves.
The U.S. needs help as well.
Our poverty index is still seen and this is much larger than 1910.
Our work force has become depressed.
Unemployment rate is on a constant rise.
We must find a vaster way to support our lives.
If we don't, we will realize that of genocide.
Think about South Africa and how we can develop an economic
union.
All that land they have can become wealth to both of us.
If we help them, they will help us.
Let's go and discover South Africa.

/

Today is no different from another.
American deficit still is in economic trouble.
Why are politicians not trying to negotiate to lower the deficit?
We do not want to cut spending but ride our deficit to a ceiling.
One would think because of ignorance.

However, this cannot be perceived this way.

Politicians are developing our future into a political-religious state.

Obscurity is what this well present because this nation will remain Church and State.

Only the religious focus will be a backdoor to cause harm to leaders who want a more godly reform.

Who is who in America will be suppressed to form a premeditated roster of success.

Profiling is what this is called.

Beware because this country of people has been warned.

World War III has been treated as an individual utilized to international relate when her life is at stake.

This will stop another world war but how do you believe that the facility of life encrypted is what is needed to protect us, when wrong is being done by hurting her?

World War III is our bed pillow as well as our front door.

May I suggest, trust in God!

/

The Civil War was the beginning of this nation's deficit.

As stated before, South Africa is our best bet.

Build up and form an economy there because that's who brought us all that money that we lost in war against ourselves.

South Africa and its people are really a treasure.

However, this time do not enslave.

Be more spiritual in your ways and when all the people of this great nation covet, South Africa will become such as the United States.

This is foreseen philosophically because to desire growth you must change from being in a whiten world and all must come together to bring this nation back to its economic standard, which is not owning another man a damn penny.

Not a red cent we have to give; only when it is to assist in depleting famine.

Leave the Middle East militia!

War has come to pass.
Famine must disappear as well.
Matthew 24:34 states: **"*VERILY I SAY UNTO YOU, THIS GENERATION [EVERY FORTY YEARS] SHALL NOT PASS, TILL ALL THESE THINGS BE FULFILLED.*"**
IT IS TIME FOR THIS NATION TO HEAL AND HELP OURSELVES.

T*H*E*E*N*D

RISE & SHINE

RISE & SHINE

Islet is cold.
Iris is not.
The moon is frozen.
The sun is hot.
The morning has come and it's time to get up.
Rise and shine my people!

Insects, Worms, and Maggots

We are insects, worms, and maggots.
Or is that maggots, insects and worms?
White seem to be first.
The colored, however, supersedes this thought.
There was slavery encapsulated.
Before, the nomads were oppressed.
And through all this suppression, white man formed his artistic
expression.
Tenant farming and sharecropping became that which manifested
through enslavement being emancipated.
The white man proclaimed that to be free meant to be undignified.
So the slaves lived in a racial environment.
Prejudice was the white man to all that was colored.
The nomads were reserved from the white's suffrage.
They were given money to live by the federal government.
However, poverty is still prevalent in their world due to prejudice
of the White man in who they are.
The white paint on the Negro face states: "*Fame and fortune will
come via my ass being licked. You must state your face is the white
man's identity. He allows you to be successful through your stated
inferiority and the white man's captured superiority.*"
The Natives trusted and allowed the white man to discover them.
Today, the Natives are the conqueror of their destiny.
Nonetheless, reserved they remain.
Dynasty is there.
The colored has overcome the white man!

Nevertheless, they seem to be ignorant of the fact and the white man lies to keep them like that.

Perception must be the reality of the color yet, they let the white man conceptualize what is real.

We are Insects, Worms, and Maggots.

Great Lines

Soft tissue is the kind to use.
Hard tissue bruises.
Wipe your eyes when you grieve.
Bereavement is at hand.
Issues are the tissue you have.

A wax floor is slippery.
If you fall, I hope you don't sustain any injuries.
Wipe your eyes as a child.
Let them know you are not to grown to cry.
This floor hurt and now I am really hurting inside.

A ball was thrown to you by a car.
You dodge it to defeat being scarred.
However, then a punch was swung for someone other than
yourself.
You couldn't dodge that.
A concussion you have.

Gesturing, you beacon for a friend.
He ignored you because he was with someone else.
You knew this was called a status quo.
You told him later he acted like he did not know you.
Your feelings were hurt but you hid this well.
Now you and this friend aren't speaking.

The tester of your faith stands in illumination.
So well lit you said she might persuade you.
A shining example she would make.
Would you cheat and become hated?
You did deceive but you did it your way.

Take advantage of what is there.
Achieve the ultimate right when you can.

Dupe those who are wrong.
Stand as tall as tall is.
A trick is never a treat to give.

Inspiration is red hot.
Encourage those who are not.

Baby Boy

He was so strong.
He knew I was stuck.
When he loved, he stuttered.
He wore a gold tooth.
He dresses as most Negros does.
His Mom called him Baby Boy.
He talked real well if you listen to him.
When you didn't, he knew he did not make sense.
That's when he would grit his teeth.
The gold one would shine at night and therefore, you would listen because it hurt your eyes.
Once you heard what he said, his gold tooth would stop shining.
The most ridiculous thing and if you laugh, he would become sensitive.
So you tendered to ask: "*Baby Boy why your tooth glows that way*?"
He states: "*Don't fuck with me. Don't fuck with my mouth. Female, I'll knock you out! You think you can talk about me and love me to. I don't think so. And by the way, I don't play.*
Now, I have learned to laugh, because he says it might just be funny to me.
His memory is not there, so I ask: "*What do you mean*?"
He states, real intelligently: "*I am silly it seems.*"
One day we were together and he saw some friends.
He stops to talk and to see what they were getting in.
One guy stated he was going to get high.
That's when Carlos, nicknamed Baby Boy, started to talk more clear and concise.
I said to myself, I thought he had speech impairment.
However, it has gotten better.
Why has his voice cleared up!
Then, that is when I discovered what I did not know.
Baby Boy was not the same and the guy asked him to take me home and come back around eight.

He turns to look at me.

That's when I saw he was missing his gold tooth.

Why does he wear that gold when it causes him so much trouble in speech?

It is because his face changes and he is no longer the strong handsome man I see.

So, I step out the car and stated I will walk home.

*"No, **need to worry Baby Boy.**
I let you just be with your enjoyment."*

Easy way to call it quits.

Even the muscles had shrunk, which means Baby Boy was no longer a hunk.

WHY TRUST?

Love? But he always hurt you. Can't leave the punk? But he is abusive. In too deep? Just leave him!

Alone? Isn't that the best way to be? Need someone to lean on? But the world is crazy. Want to share your thoughts? Just pray to the Lord!

Joe you wrong. The color woman was suppressed by the white man for too long.

And now you want to fight. I dare you to strike me like that. Why do I trust? Any man today is a wrongdoer!

Intimacy? But you should want to be free. Need to be loved? But you just end a relationship with a no good thug. Want comfort? Why not find you a support group!

Depressed? Isn't by yourself a way to think. Need someone to talk to? But people are not true. Desire a best friend? I am always here!

Steven isn't good for moral support. He will seek you for sex and enjoyment. You say you are depressed and stressed from to many bad relationships. Why do you want to trust without healing?

Not yourself? But that's because of what you been through. Can't find sense? But that's within reason of the pain you feel, Honey Boo. Colors? You have suffered now it is time to heal. Want to go out? That's it! Learn to help yourself.

The world can be deep. In depth you become to the life you live. No time to hide what you feel. Maybe a day to cry and then go out and chill!

Want a drink? Not so fast. Want to drown your sorrows as usual? No time for addiction or developing bad habits. Trust your instincts and know things will get better!

It is a sad thing to see a friend become a substance abuser. You know what is wrong but can't do nothing at all but tell him or her to not drink to solve any issue.

If you find that they are strong, you know they have listened.

Want to scream? Why not do that to let out the steam? This will help you to cope and not make a mistake to trust before you know him. Want to smile? Just smile!

You also seem to desire affection. You say this would be just a simple friend that cannot go against you. But you don't state whether that is me. I am best kept as it seems.

Let's sing and sing. Let's enjoy the life we live. Must you trust your heart with somebody? You don't. Just wait until the time has come.

You can be by yourself for a while. If you need a smile, humor your mind.

Never letting anyone in and then before you know it you have met the prefect man.

Why trust when you can be free? Why need anybody?

Love is true to those who define true meaning.

Why trust when he is misleading?

Download

I am going on a trip because I need to spend a week away from this concept.
Don't burn that money.
Don't waste it either.
I'll spend it on something that I dislike.
It may be a venture but since I have spent my money, I can get high.
Clip art is my drawings and they are of beautiful megabits.
I think I am superfly so I play Rock & Roll all night.
Madness sheer excitement escape to the highest heights of my imagination is when I know who I am and where I have been and thick am I and my jeans are tight.
With my big tits, I walk as if I am filled with sexual desire.
I see myself and smile.
Oh shit, I'm feeling something that is so real.
I know if I lost focus, I lose my inner being.
So I give self a damn bulge and know that this is my world and therefore, I don't lose the sensation.
The impression I give is that of confidence.
Self-asserted and assured, I moving up to finer things.
Handsome is the day and the night falls so lovely.
But I need to see what's mine.
I need to see what belongs to me.
Strikingly, I find that I own so many priceless images.
A landscape I may pick to be serenity.
Or, a portrait is nice for the stillness.
I'll plant a flower field to enjoy the contentment.
Equanimity is a silent panic.
I am just a being of the higher intelligence.
The noise is a clamor that does not last.
I will be the uproar of happiness.
Such a pleasure to have told you this.
If you want a replica, you may do the same.
That is joy in a virtual domain.

No more is the chance than any other government.
I have ruled this empire as long as I can remember.
Direction is easy to follow.
If you fail, I will not fail mines because all are downloadable.
I do not share my empirical secrets.
I am a régime of systems.
Simulated by thoughts that are pure.
Only I can be the downloader.

SOME MORE POETRY I HAVE TO GIVE. LISTEN!

/

If I was to give this a title, it would not make sense.
You see this is simply about self.
It tells about what I stand for.
Representation of our history and that we are making as I speak.
Just today I was watching television and media was telling, as usually, the perils of the world.
I said to self this is a never ending story.
A boy killed a girl and the body was discovered.
They had been looking for her for several years.
Finally, she was found mutilated and buried under leaves in rural Mississippi.
He had told officials that she was missing.
No one knew of their conflictions, therefore, the boy was not suspected.
Nonetheless, they had to investigate and three years later she was found and forensics established his blood pathogen.
Nevertheless, he had left Iowa and moved.
Nobody knew his whereabouts and thus, a girl has lost her life and her lover is the fugitive at large.
Will law enforcement ever find this boy?

A crime is always a historical event in the criminal justice system.

A man embezzled millions of dollars from the company he worked for.
A woman assisted him in doing the accounting.
They did this for many years.
At this company both made six figure salaries and they had the majority of the power.
Therefore, they controlled the money allocations.
They increased their salaries via a constructed result.
Both are gone on to other jobs without being caught.

But one day documentation was found that this money had been
taken from a secret account.
How this was done nobody has reveal yet.
Wherefore, the woman and man are still free-world convicts.
Proof must come forth on how they did this!

The penal code is known by many; however, law enforcement
cannot do a thing if the proof isn't in it.

In truth I stand, here and now, representing a system of reform and
elements erected in which adjudication is placed on the streets and in
that sense, if you have committed crime do not believe you have
depleted my complexity.
I am the criminal justice system.

>

The stars at night shine a certain brightness that evades humanity
and without additional lighting, mankind cannot perceive surroundings
appropriately.

A volcano erupts and the sky is on fire.
My eyes look as far as they can see.
I am not along.
I stand in a crowd asking is this a scene or reality.
The reality of it all is the image of a volcano and the scene became
the crowd enjoying the fireworks.
This was a holiday for us.
Little did we know our lives were at stake!
The earth shook and the blessing of it all was that many of us
were outside and therefore, no one was killed.
The magnitude of the quake was a 9.0 and the sink hole that it
created became a water fall.

)(

The sound juddered with vibrating effect.
In the effervescent, the statue manifest.
As dull as grey can be but as warm as its coloring, the cat eyes
sparkled staring and scaring me.
I trembled, quite afraid.
I had been here for so long that I was in a wobbled state.
No one seemed to be here at all, not even an animal.
But just that moment the gray cat appeared and I found that
somewhat comforting.
I said to self: "***Well, I am not in the wild.
People have live here, sometime.
However, this land is in a barren state and I am here agitated.***"
The grey cat rubbed my leg telling me she was the head.
I begin to follow her to where she went and she took me to where
she lived.
Where I had been used to be a small town, which these people left
to form a more grandeur place and I am here to be their slave.

][

Magnificent I am.
I am who I say I am.
If I am not, then who are you?
I barely ever meet new people to confuse.
I am what I am and that is not you.
I see you say that you are [*my*] self and that is intimate.
However, you can exist as an oval for me to have when I do not
want to be involved with man.
Let him fuck you as if you have my ass.
Girlfriend, I really don't give a damn.

}{
They say they adore me every time they represent bad.

Why do they appear to want to kick my ass?
Have I sprung them with my defenses?
Have I taken their senses?
Then they come as if I am the one afraid when it's them that are
being played.
If you can take my life, jump for.
If you can cause me pain, leap.
If you want me harmed, skip how come.
Just do it!
When all this has been done, don't you be the one gone.
No warning, just acknowledgement that must be put there.
And, know this, this is not a dare.
Just beware!

**

Provocation is the estimation of ornateness.
Taunting yourself can be a venture.
Don't gamble that love is in it.
As a sexual challenge, is love necessitated?
Defy what you feel.
Be so bold, you will know if he's for real.
And if you find that he is not.
Let go and find someone else.

%%*

Maximum exposure is never for what it shows.
The life exploited has more outrage to unclose.
Why not define yourself in what has been shown?
Then you repute them with your stance of I am grown.
From there they well know that gossip is just sycophancy.
They talk because they want to get into your panties.
Why do they call you a whore?
Say, who's telling it has never been up my oval.

Is that the problem by me being so scandalous?
Your lust is not part of my attraction.
Indignity never discredits anyone when it is all about who you are holding intimately in your arms!
I just don't want [*to fuck*] the media.

$*$

I am asked as much as I am told.
The feeling I gave is that I don't know.
This never achieves what it should.
I am to tell them what I couldn't.
Do I make believe that I know?
Do I say that this is what I'm told?
Or, should I just say nothing at all?
The usual response is to speak as if you asked them something.
Confusion is accomplished and therefore, you have told them nothing.

!!*

I am as much as I think I am.
If I do not believe I am worthy, I am less then all mankind.
I travel this journey to define self.
If I am told that I am meaningless, I do not listen.
This is not sound advice.
Who tells this is trying to hinder my stride.
I step with a more definite purpose and know that God guides my focus.
And therefore, my leadership is mine and the negativity belongs to Jehovah.
God's Hell is open.

..*

Brother, I'm going to write my poetry!

Who told you your intonation can discourage me?
Not your silly rapping dissuades a thing.
My poetry becomes preventive measures for humanity to treasure.
Therefore, I encourage you to try.
You'll help me make the world right.

Sister, why the scowling face?
My poetry makes you think the right way.
It is for women's health.
I am just trying to get you there.
To a different level that is.
All I ask is that you keep it real, which this will become your reality.
However, if it affects my life, it will not be daunting.
Frighteningly, I hope you confront me.
Nonetheless, I know it will be indirect.
If it is not, then I know how to handle this.
I'll tell you what I said and maybe this will set your ass off.
Sister, remember whatever happens, you are the cause.
A confrontational bitch is always at fault.

??*

*Now this poetry piece is finished but this isn't the end of it.
Poetry is too splendid!* **DARK SUN**

THE FALL OF ROME

Double jeopardy
Close call
Skit roll
Warns us all
That we must make our existence a fulfillment or the economy will
fall.
You all know that's what happened to Rome.
And therefore, we must care for our own.

Just a struggle and lot of strife
Fast pace trying to manage life
Looking out for self is the individualize thought.
This will bring a greater worth and disengage another catastrophic
default.
The Fall of Rome will not be within this.
I am successful and that's the way it is.

In a runt
Short of money
Just a rat race
I'll overcome my financial troubles!
No evasion for nonpayment and ducking out has been disabled.
What am I to do to alleviate the stress is a hanging question that
has manifested.
The Fall of Rome is in sight.
Nonetheless, I'll wait until it happens.

Liquid wets the surface.
As the picture forms in the moonlit, the canvas of eyes glows.
The artist has not finished what her mind unfolds.
However, that is not what is foretold.

The eyes belong to Dark Sun.

The artist is swift with her brush.
Her hand strokes the canvas with a decisive touch.
Yet, she does not know what will come of this.
No visual image is represented.

The eyes of Dark Sun stand in silence.

This spiritual healer is the artist talents.
Faster she has become.
The picture is still forming.

Dark Sun is within the mural and once the artist finishes, she
would not believe she did this.

Only with an abstract in her mind, a beautiful figure is defined.
The artist has done this before and therefore, her masterpiece is
known as:

DARK SUN

FIDELITY

Resplendent is my spirit and my soul is transcendent.
My temperament is cored by strength.
I do not know why I am exposed to others weaknesses but God has shown me why I am a true leader.
Naturally my mind develops the mood.
Emotional I may become but sentiments must be from things of importance.
In darkness, I pace and I must face what the world conviction is.
I am DARK SUN and I devote my song with confidence.
Assurance is the trust and reliance I have in self.
Loyalty to oneself is a commitment mandated by God [*to who you are*].
Allegiance I pledge and on pillars I stand voicing who I am and the image is invigorating.
From a distance I hear someone calling me and I turn to answer.
"**DARK SUN**," he yells.
I say, "**I am here!**"
He finds me and we make love.

THE BEGINNING

DO MORE TO GET MORE

The prophecy of humanity states that we must work together to
achieve abundance and prosperity.
Mankind today does not work toward ending disparity, however,
work for individual parity.
We must do more to get more.
We must build a bridge of consensus to grow.
If we do not, the world is apparently in a manifold.
Meaning, the diversity of the United States requires us to know
what's at stake.
When we are not working together to achieve for all, everyone will
lose out.
So let's stand as one and become more powerful.

YOU WILL KNOW

Life is a focus within humanity.
As you live, you must see what it means.
If you sense a need to help, you just might be a leader created for greatness.
If you feel a need to know, you just might depart with knowledge unknown.
If there is suggestion that gets your attention, you may just become a prime minister.
When you know what your artistic expression maintains, you may become famous.
When your fortune is foretold, your insight will disclose who you will become.
If none of these things are a variable, you lack focus and your reflection will be your soul.
In all, you will know.

I*N/P*R/A*Y/E*R

Lord God Jehovah, remove this trouble from my life.

Many days I have wiped the tears from my eyes.

This struggle and strife I am in is not mine.

I have been wrongfully deeded by mankind.

As I pray that you have my back and that you are the strength vested in life, I know that you are much more and therefore, I have no worries.

I will trust in God.

You gave me a destiny to fulfill.

I truly will and mankind will adhere to the prophecy I am in.

When I win Lord, I will remember the greatness you told me I would achieve at an early age and thus, Lord, as I live today, I see this greatness being created.

I own grace and honor to you Lord and not man who tries to dissuade me that I have no right to life and his or hers is greater than mine.

I close now *Jehovah* and say *HALLELUJAH AMEN*!

//*/*/*

My mind Lord is heavy.

I am so tired of mankind doing wrong.

If I could only depart with the knowledge needed, the world would not be gone.

Their minds are destroyed from disease of what they cannot achieve.

The norms of society have been embedded throughout humanity.

Why does man believe he can change them Lord?

The norms Lord!

You are the one who told us via your Ten Commandments what was right and what was wrong.

Why does mankind continue to steal, kill, and lie is only known in their disbelief in a Divine Order – *Jehovah God Lord*!

It seems Lord that I am the only one concerned with Deity.

All of humanity defines Christianity before they praise God [*Lord Jehovah*].

I must continue to be true to **Acts 20:21** and serve you Jehovah.

Your son is my salvation and purgatory into Heaven.

Jesus Christ Lord answers and defines my life in the world as a carrier of his Father's word.

Therefore, Lord I bow my head and bend my knees in prayer and know that you are there.

AMEN

//*/*/*

Today I come to you Lord in the most humble way.

I know blessings are given and troubles are only a memory [*from yesterday*].

My purpose is stated in my experiences and my experiences have provided my purpose.

Lord, I know you know why you love me.

Mankind may not be for me.

Through your grace Lord, you honor my life with your voice and via mind I listen.

Jehovah God Lord is the master of my soul and spirit has been formed because you are *The Almighty God*.

HALLELUJAH

//*/*/*/*

I come today Lord as I am.

I am trying my best to eradicate sin but man wants to hinder me.

I will not feel that repentance can help until I am clear of what has already happen.

And Lord, that is within my blessings.

I know Lord that you want the best for me and therefore, my enemies will recede into a damn pit you may have for them or just not where they can cause me any penalties.

In all Lord, I am who you say I should be and that is your creature amongst humanity.

To *Jehovah God Lord* I give the highest praise and say,

HALLELUJAH AMEN!

+++++++

I know Lord that I am set in my ways.

The concept of man is not a transition I am in but Lord your guidance would help immensely.

I Lord view life through lens of structure and systems.

I am within the world and I am of God and therefore, *Lord God Jehovah*, mankind states I must be destroyed.

However, to be destroyed in this world, I must have an affliction and/or an addiction.

For this reason Lord, humanity only destroys themselves and fulfillment to them is only a superficial existence.

Yet they threaten me with ascertain destruction but not death.

Lord, I cannot be in the world with someone living the life I should and thus, allay I have become and my patience is even more stronger in which I pray to you Lord and know with a certainty solace will be delivered.

In all Lord, I will close and say you are the keeper of my soul.

Hallelujah Amen!

*****

Lord in the light of your blessings I am.

And in spite of what man states, you are the tester of my faith.

I do believe in you Father as my greater existence and Lord you quench my thirst.

And for that reason, I am doing your Godly work.

I know Lord without you I would not be.

Therefore, I trust in *The* and never do I sway my trust in those that say they have a greater [self] worth.

No one is more worthy than you, Lord, and unto you Father, I offer my Psalms.

I pray that you contend my soul so that temptation is not my foe.

Thus, I say to you Lord that you are *The Almighty God* and greater be my existence in this world because I am made from your bosom and molded by your palms.

Hallelujah!

****

This is a day the Lord gave.

I am blessed to be in your presence Jehovah.

My prayers are now daily spoken.

I write as if they are part of my soul in which prayer develops my inner core.

Holistic I have become and you are my solution.

I know I am worthy of your crown in Heaven and therefore, I bow my head and say

AMEN

+++++++++++++

This bread that nourishes self is fulfilling my belly.

This meat that satisfies my hunger is nourishment with added nutrients.

But Father the non-edible food that you share with my soul is just as much and many times I have felt it to be more fulfilling.

I am preparing my temple for my transition home and in transgression I live with your spirit within my soul.

To you I am because your Son is my salvation.

With sacrament I am within my faith and by grace you wash me in the blood of lamb.

To *The Almighty God*, I come as I am!

Hallelujah Amen

****

Lord you are my help and support.

Without you I could not start my morning into a fulfilling day.

I ask you and you do provide my blessings continuously.

As I pray to you for a cleansing of souls in which you well speak to other souls, I know the world well become more Godly profound and the problems that plague us well be beaten down.

The status of the world is left up to you Lord but Lord I will do my best in serving you.

Departing your word to the multitude, my life will glow a righteous glow because I want the world to know you are the keeper of my soul.

To you Lord my life is worthy and I will live in the mist of your grace and honor you day by day.

In all, I say glory be thou name.

Hallelujah Amen!

))))))))))))))))))))))V((((((((((((((((((((

I do not wonder Lord that you know that you are the master of my soul and therefore, I live a righteous life so that in my darkness hour I will remain whole.

Even when my enemies are many and my friends are few, you are the keeper of my soul and my defenses when I cannot see through these inequities.

Within your bosom I am and throughout the world you prepare me to be amidst hatred and crime.

Thus far Lord, your mighty power has shielded me from any harm because I am protected by the armor of God and therefore, I will be justly rewarded.

The Almighty God is the shelter of my spirit and the guardian of my soul and defends me because I am the carrier of his word.

In all Lord, I close and say righteously

AMEN!

)))))))))))))))))))))))))A(((((((((((((((((((((((

Starting today Lord, my outlook on life is that of grand and splendor [*splendor* and *grand*].

I am glad to be of service to you and your Commandments Lord.

I live as righteous as your Word say I should and your glory is a brilliance understood.

Humility is modesty in the aura of your grace.

I do not pretend that I am saved but your salvation is gaited.

I walk down a virtuous path and I honor you with moral and truth.

And therefore Lord, I offer my soul to you.

AMEN WITH THE HIGHEST PRIASE – HALLELUJAH!

{{{{{{{{{{{{{{{{{{{{{{{{{{{{{{△{{{{{{{{{{{{{{{{{{{{{{{{{{{{{{{{{{{{

Lord I tried my best but it did not work out.

I tried to provide the people with the needed insight but they did not listen and said you are no one.

But Lord I will not give-up and hopefully they will give-in, if this not so, then the demons will win.

I came to you today Lord to share my thoughts.

In all, it will not be my fault.

When this City of fools find-out that law must prevail, the demons of Hell will be in their heads.

I pray to you Lord that you can forgive and therefore, your judgment will because I do not want to be the one you send revenge but if I am, I shall do as commanded.

With all said Lord, I will become worthy of your honor and do as you did in Sodom and Gomorrah.

The Cities shall be laced with your grace and glory and this will be *The Almighty God* modern day story and not one of perils that mankind knows.

May the sun shine once more on prophesy of soul!

Destiny is never foretold.

AMEN!

****EPILOGUE****EPILOGUE****EPILOGUE****

"Surely you live, you must die!"

Life is promise to no one.

Death is for all of us.

"Surely you live, you must die!"

[Wherefore, life is to live and life must demise.]